Relief from Headache

Relief from Headache

by

Donald I. Peterson, M.D.

Published and Distributed by

WARREN H. GREEN
8356 Olive Blvd
St. Louis, MO 63132

Copyright © 1983, 1990, and 2005 by Donald I. Peterson, M.D.

All rights reserved. This book is protected by copyright. No part of this book may be reproduced or transmitted in any form or by any means, electronic or mechanical, including photocopying, recording, or by any informational storage or retrieval system without permission in writing from the publisher.

World Rights Reserved

Library of Congress Catalog Card Number: 2005925243

ISBN 0-87527-547-8

First Edition 1983
Second Edition 1990
Third Edition 2005

Printed in the United States of America

Cover illustration by Bonnie Wallace

To my wife Elsie

who spent many hours transcribing and proofreading the manuscript for this book and who undoubtedly would have suffered from both "transcription headache" and "proofreading headache" had she not used the method of headache management described in these pages.

Preface

Millions of people suffer from headache. Most of them have been unable to find effective relief because the commonly used methods of headache management provide only symptomatic relief and they fail to remove the cause of this troublesome symptom. There are many causes for headache. These include life threatening conditions such as brain tumors, hemorrhages, infections, and also severe emotional disturbances. Most people who suffer from headache do not have any of these conditions, but rather they suffer from common kinds of headache often referred to as migraine and muscle-contraction headache. Pain killing drugs are the most frequently used form of headache therapy, but they provide only temporary benefit. Other kinds of headache treatment including acupuncture, biofeedback, and several other forms of therapy may give help in a few cases but they are not very effective for the majority of people and they are expensive.

This book provides information about a very successful approach to the management of common headache. This method of treatment is simple, effective, and inexpensive. The reason it is so successful is that its objective is that of getting rid of the abnormalities that cause headache rather than only providing symptomatic relief. This method of treatment can provide relief in up to 90 percent of headache victims.

Many kinds of headache including those due to serious disease are discussed in this book, but these pages have been written especially for those persons who do not have serious disease who need a simple, effective, inexpensive means of overcoming headache.

Donald I. Peterson, M.D.

Contents

1. Headache – Man's Most Common Pain..................................1
2. How to Get Relief from Common Headache.....................25
3. Muscle Spasm in the Neck and Scalp Can Cause Headache...61
4. Chronic Headache Following Head and Neck Injury.......79
5. Brain Tumors Can Cause Headache..................................87
6. Headache Due to Hemorrhage Inside the Head.............95
7. Headache Can Be Caused by Infections........................108
8. Migraine: There are Several Kinds.................................115
9. Classic Migraine (Migraine With Aura).........................121
10. Common Migraine (Migraine Without Aura)................144
11. Cluster Headache and Other Uncommon Forms of Head Pain...150
12. Headache Associated With Mental Illness....................157
13. Headache Associated With Systemic Disease...............166
14. Headache Caused by Abnormalities of the Eyes, Ears, Nose, Sinuses and Teeth, and the Cranial Neuralgias....175
15. Other Kinds of Headache..187
16. Effects and Side Effects of Drugs Used to Treat Headache..202

1

Headache – Man's Most Common Pain

Headache in ancient history.

Headache is one of the most common pains that plagues mankind and it is likely that this has been true throughout our entire history. Several references to this common problem found in ancient literature support this view. Hippocrates called headache a "heaviness of the head."[1] Galen referred to headache localized to one side of the head and called it "hemicrania," a term that is used occasionally even today for migraine.[2] But since Galen considered this condition to be fatal it is unlikely that he was referring to migraine headache when he used this term. He further believed that headache was caused by "black bile" on the brain. Plato showed laudable insight when he observed that there was a relationship between headache and emotions.[3] It is true, however, that references to headache in ancient and Renaissance literature are rather few. The reasons for this may be that prior to recent times there was little success in gaining an understanding of the many causes for headache or in treating it successfully.

RELIEF FROM HEADACHE

Some think headache is a more serious problem in these modern days of high stress and life in the fast lane than it was in ancient times. Don't you believe it. The following words are said to come from a Mesopotamian incantation dating back to the 4000–3000 B.C. period:

> Headache roameth over the desert, blowing
> > like the wind,
> Flashing like lightning, it is loosed above and below;
> It cutteth off like a reed, him, who fearest not his god;
> Like a stalk of henna it slitteth his thews.
> It wasteth the flesh of him who hath no
> > protecting goddess,
> Flashing like a heavenly star, it cometh like the dew;
> It standeth hostile against the wayfarer,
> > scorching him like the day.
> This man it hath struck and
> Like one with heart disease he staggereth,
> Like one bereft of reason he is broken,
> Like that which has been cast into the fire
> > he is shrivelled,
> Like a wild ass . . . his eyes are full of cloud,
> On himself he feedeth, bound in death;
> Headache whose course like the dread
> > windstorm none knoweth,
> None knoweth its full time or its bond.

These words show that headache was probably just as serious a problem for people who lived in ancient times as it is for us today.

Shakespeare mentioned headache. The following comes from *Othello*, III, iii. 287:

> *Desdemona.* Why do you speak so faintly?

HEADACHE—MAN'S MOST COMMON PAIN

> Are you not well?
> *Othello.* I have a pain upon my forehead here.
> *Desdemona.* ... Let me but bind it hard, within this hour. It will be well.

The following words come from *Romeo and Juliet*, II, v. 48:

> Lord, how my head aches! What a head have I!
> It beats as it would fall in twenty pieces.

Headache is a common problem.

The frequency and seriousness of headache in the general population cannot be accurately stated; but it is estimated that in any given year 50 to 90 percent of people have this symptom. Ziegler and associates found that 50 percent of men and women within the United States have experienced "severe" or "disabling" headaches at some time in their lives.[4] It is true that some persons deny ever hav-

Used with the kind permission of Carnrick Laboratories, Inc.

Figure 1. Can't somebody do something about these terrible headaches? It's a dog's life to have to suffer like this.

ing had a headache but on the other hand many people are partially incapacitated or totally disabled by this problem. Well-known historical persons who are reported to have suffered from severe headache include Thomas Jefferson, Ulysses S. Grant, Sigmund Freud, Charles Darwin, Lewis Carroll, and D. H. Lawrence.[5]

Headache is a common symptom with which patients present to physicians' offices and to hospital emergency rooms. Those who seek professional medical attention may account for only a small portion of the total headache population (Figure 1). It is likely that the majority of persons who suffer from this condition treat themselves with simple pain-killing drugs such as aspirin, Anacin, Excedrin, Tylenol, Advil, and similar medications, rather than seeking treatment from physicians. Countless others who have sought professional medical help in the past treat themselves by various methods because the professional help that they have received has not been effective.

The huge quantity of analgesic medication used throughout the world is an indication of the frequency and seriousness of the headache problem. Approximately twelve thousand tons of aspirin are consumed annually in the United States alone.[6] This would allow each person in this country to use one hundred fifty tablets each year. In addition, large amounts of other kinds of analgesics such as Tylenol are used. It is reported that sales of Tylenol and other preparations of acetaminophen account for 35 percent of the "over-the-counter" analgesic market. Not all of these simple analgesic preparations are used for the treatment of headache, but it is well known that a large portion of them are used for this purpose.

HEADACHE—MAN'S MOST COMMON PAIN

What causes headache?

There are many causes for headache. These range from serious, life-threatening conditions (such as meningitis, brain tumor, brain abscess, and hemorrhage) to prolonged neck muscle contraction and the common cold. Fortunately the great majority of headaches are not related to any serious disease but are serious only because of the pain and inconvenience they cause.

The severity of headache may have little relationship to the seriousness of its cause. Headaches due to brain tumor or meningitis may be excruciating; yet, on some occasions headaches due to these conditions are relatively mild and cannot be compared in severity to the headache of a migraine attack or a hangover. Cluster headache, which is considered to be a variant of migraine, is one of the most severe types of headache. It is so severe that it makes some of those who have it feel like committing suicide. Yet cluster headache is not a dangerous condition; it is serious only because of the severe pain it causes. In the general population headaches due to serious life-threatening conditions are few in number while millions of people suffer from headaches that may be equally painful even though no serious disease is present. Other headaches that can cause severe pain but which are not caused by serious disease include muscle-contraction headache (also called myofacial headache), headache associated with viral infections, menstrual headaches, and most headaches following injuries to the head and neck.

Headache is not a disease but rather it is a symptom of disease or evidence of some abnormal body function. The causes for headaches resulting from life-threatening conditions such as brain tumors, meningitis, and intracranial hemorrhage are quite well known; but the causes of the more common types of headaches such as migraine and muscle-contraction headache which make up the majority of all headaches in the general population are poorly understood.

Even though the causes for the common kinds of headache are not very well known, it has been well established which structures (both inside and outside the head) are pain-sensitive and are thus capable of producing headache. Most people who have headache believe this symptom is due to some abnormality inside the head, but this usually is not true. The majority of headaches arise from abnormalities in structures outside the skull. Some kinds of headache, such as classic migraine and headaches associated with viral infections, may arise from pain-sensitive tissues both inside and outside the skull.

All parts of the body with which we are familiar by means of touch and observations are sensitive to pain, and the same can be said of all tissues of the head and neck that are outside the skull. These include skin, muscles, nerves, blood vessels, ligaments, and other fibrous tissue, as well as organs such as the eyes, ears, nose, and sinuses. Headache, or head pain, can result from abnormalities in any of these structures. By contrast, most of the structures inside the skull — including most of the brain tissue, most of the coverings of the brain, most of the blood vessels and some of the nerves — are not pain-sensitive. Therefore they cannot be the source of headache. This insensitivity of most of the intracranial structures can be demonstrated during neurosurgical operations, some of which can be done while the patient is awake. Most of the brain, for example, can be cut, cauterized, crushed, or injured in various other ways without causing any discomfort. However, it has been reported that some structures deep inside the brain are pain sensitive. The three kinds of intracranial tissues listed below are pain-sensitive.

(1) Portions of the large intracranial blood vessels can be the source of headache. These include the large arteries at the base of the brain, the main blood vessels which supply the dura which covers the brain and also the veins and draining venous sinuses through which blood flows as it leaves the brain, but not the other intracranial blood vessels.

(2) Some portions of the meninges (this is the name given to the protective coverings of the brain) are pain-sensitive, but most of the meninges have no sensory nerves or pain-sensitive nerve endings. Like the brain itself, most of these tissues are not a source of pain or headache even if they are being destroyed by tumors, infections, or other kinds of serious diseases.

(3) The intracranial portions of the fifth, ninth, and tenth cranial nerves are pain-sensitive. The other cranial nerves are either not sensitive to stimuli that characteristically produce discomfort in pain-sensitive tissues or they make a minor contribution to the sensation of pain and production of headache.

The fifth cranial nerve carries pain sensation from all the pain-sensitive structures inside the head above the tentorium. The tentorium is a tent-shaped structure composed of thick, tough tissue separating the cerebral hemispheres above from the cerebellum and brain stem below. The pain-sensitive structures inside the head that lie below the tentorium are supplied by the sensory divisions of the ninth and tenth cranial nerves which enter the brain stem and also the upper cervical nerves that enter the upper portion of the spinal cord. These structures include portions of the large blood vessels, nerves, and meninges around the brain stem and cerebellum.

Pain arising from inside the head usually occurs from (1) dilation of blood vessels; (2) stretching of pain-sensitive structures; or (3) irritation of pain-sensitive tissue by infection, hemorrhage, tumors, abscesses, or blood clots. Although the lining of the skull — called the periosteum — is pain-sensitive, the remainder of the skull has little or no sensitivity to stimuli which would cause pain in other parts of the body.

Since all structures outside the skull are pain-sensitive, headache can result from many different abnormalities of these tissues, including: infection, injury, hemorrhage, impairment of circulation, and prolonged muscle spasm. Headache may also be due to abnormalities involving the structures of the neck. It is well recognized that headache can be associated with spasm or prolonged, painful contraction of the neck muscles and fibrous tissue which can result from several causes. These include meningitis or hemorrhage inside the head, as well as abnormalities of the neck itself such as those due to disease and injury. In some cases this muscle spasm may be due to persistent muscle tension related to nervousness, fear, anxiety, or depression as well as from bad posture or just getting "up-tight." It has been long recognized that muscle spasm in muscles of the scalp and neck, regardless of its cause, may cause pain and headache in all parts of the head; but this cause of headache has often been neglected by physicians while great emphasis has been placed on headache thought to be due to abnormal dilation of blood vessels.

There has been an ongoing search for hypothetical blood-vessel-dilating substances and pain-producing substances that cause headache. If such substances were found, it could be a giant step forward in finding more successful drug treatments for some kinds of headaches. These include migraine and headaches associated with acute infections in which abnormalities of blood vessels may be partially responsible for the pain. Also included in the group are headaches due to hangover, lack of oxygen, and the effects of some toxic chemicals.

The most common kinds of headache, however, are not due to blood vessel abnormalities; rather they are those caused by painful contraction of neck and scalp muscles and fibrous tissue. These include muscle-contraction headache as well as headache associated with head and neck injuries or diseases of the cervical spine. This group also rightfully includes many headaches that in the past have been diagnosed as common migraine. A better name for these headaches is myofascial headache since most of them are caused by abnormally contracted muscles and fascia. (Fascia is one kind of fibrous tissue that holds the muscles together and in their normal position.)

There are many kinds of headache.

Headache can be classified in several different ways.

Classification of Headache

1. Vascular Headache of Migraine Type
   A. "Classic" migraine
   B. "Common" migraine
   C. "Cluster" migraine
   D. "Hemiplegic" and "Ophthalmoplegic" migraine
   E. "Lower-Half" headache
2. Muscle-Contraction Headache*
3. Combined Headache: Vascular and Muscle-Contraction
4. Headache of Nasal Vasomotor Reaction
5. Headache of Delusional, Conversion, or Hypochondriacal States
6. Nonmigrainous Vascular Headaches
7. Traction Headache
8. Headache Due to Overt Cranial Inflammation
9-13. Headache Due to Disease of Ocular, Aural, Nasal and Sinusal, Dental, or Other Cranial or Neck Structures
14. Cranial Neuritides
15. Cranial Neuralgias

*Tension headache and psychogenic headache are usually considered to be synonyms for muscle-contraction headaches.

Figure 2. Classification of Headache suggested by the Committee on Classification of Headache of the National Institute of Neurological Disease and Blindness of the National Institutes of Health.[8]

The classification that is most commonly used in the United States is one suggested in the early 1960s by the Committee on Classification of Headache of the National Institute of Neurological Diseases and Blindness (Figure 2). Some classifications are more detailed in that they have more categories, but in general most currently used ones are similar. They are based on what are considered to be the various causes for headache. An important feature of these classifications is the separation of vascular headaches of the migraine type from the headache due to other causes.

A recently proposed classification of headache by the

HEADACHE—MAN'S MOST COMMON PAIN

Headache Classification Committee of the International Headache Society lists over 100 kinds of headache.[7] Some headache sufferers are quite sure they have had all of them.

This classification changes the term classic migraine to migraine with aura and common migraine to migraine without aura. It lists several other rare forms of migraine.

Authorities disagree about classification and cause of common headache.

The usefulness and validity of some aspects of currently used classifications have been questioned. There are several kinds of headache that do not fit into any of these categories very well. These include headaches related to some systemic diseases, headaches due to withdrawal from drugs, those due to toxic substances, and also those that follow head injuries. An even more important question about these classifications is whether there is any valid difference between common migraine and muscle-contraction headache which is also called myofascial headache. Some authorities would draw a sharp line of differentiation between these two kinds of headache. They believe "vascular" headaches, including common migraine, are due to abnormal dilation of blood vessels — which is probably related to some pain producing chemical. They think muscle-contraction headaches are due to emotional problems. Muscle-contraction headache, tension headache, and also psychogenic headache are terms that are believed by some physicians to be synonymous. They are usually incorrectly believed to be due only to nervousness, depression, anger, hostility, or frustration and therefore are caused by emotional factors rather than by chemical or physiological abnormalities as is thought to be the cause for migraine.

Painful, contracted neck muscles that cause headache can in some cases be related to emotional stress and nervous tension. But there is no evidence that most people who have headache from tight neck muscles are any more nervous than their more fortunate associates who do not have headache. There are also many other causes for tight neck muscles. Tender, contracted neck muscles frequently result from various uncomfortable head and neck positions and bad posture which in turn cause muscle strain. These occur in some occupations that require constant forward flexion of the head and neck or frequent and persistent turning of the head. Other causes for tender, contracted neck muscles and headache include head and neck injuries and diseases of the neck, including arthritis, herniated intervertebral discs, infections, and occasionally tumors.

The traditional classifications of headache place common migraine and muscle-contraction headache in different categories. Common migraine by its association with classic migraine is given a respectable status because it is thought to be due to some chemical or physiological abnormality of blood vessels. Muscle-contraction headache, on the other hand, by being made synonymous with psychogenic headache by many physicians is often considered unjustifiably to be less worthy of attention. Patients who are given this diagnosis are thought by some to be less emotionally stable than those who have migraine. In addition, this headache is often considered to be less painful than the headache of those who "suffer" from migraine. Unfortunately, many people who have common muscle-contraction headache suffer in two ways. They suffer from the headache and they also experience lack of concern and sympathy from their associates and even from their doctors who often believe that they are just nervous or emotionally upset.

It has never been demonstrated that blood vessel abnormalities cause common migraine. Furthermore, there is little or no difference in the amount of neck muscle contraction in common migraine and muscle-contraction headache.[9] Persons with either of these headaches have similar emotional problems. The same drugs and other forms of treatment can be used with similar success to treat both kinds of headache. Unfortunately, current methods of treatment are not very effective for either of them even though good temporary symptomatic relief may be achieved by these means. If headaches are present daily or continuously, they are more likely to be diagnosed as muscle-contraction headache; while if they occur at less-frequent intervals, and especially if they are associated with nausea and vomiting, they are more likely to be diagnosed as migraine.

Muscle-contraction headache will be discussed in detail in chapter 3. Migraine in its various forms will be considered in chapters 8, 9, 10, and 11. Headache following head and neck injury is discussed in chapter 4.

Raskin and Appenzeller, who are authorities on diagnosis and treatment of headache, state, "The traditional classification of the commonest recurring headaches into the tension and migraine types is open to challenge."[10] As more research on headache is done, it is becoming more apparent that there may be no significant differences between common migraine and muscle-contraction headache. These headaches may be part of a continuum which also includes other kinds of headache — even classic migraine. Some headaches that are classified in the common migraine group probably are variants of classic migraine, but the great majority are more like muscle-contraction or myofascial headaches than they are like vascular headaches. Drummond and Lance found no headache characteristics that clearly differentiated between migraine and tension headache.[11]

Other headache authorities, including Dalessio who revised the well-known book entitled *Wolff's Headache and Other Head Pain*, do not agree.[12] He regrets this tendency in the last few years on the part of some physicians and authorities on headache to lump various types of headache together and "murmur of a continuum." He thinks this lack of precision is confusing the issue. Yet Wolff's famous book, which Dalessio edited, lumps together as variants of migraine many other kinds of headache that certainly are not appropriately included in that category. It includes in the migraine group such headaches as "menstrual headache; relaxation headache; Sunday headache; week-end headache; vacation headache; ordinary or common headache; menopausal headache; spring headache; summer headache; fall headache; winter headache; humidity headache; barometric headache; hot-weather headache; tropical headache; wash-day headache; cleaning-day headache; inventory headache; constipation headache; indigestion headache; sick headache; bilious headache; and so forth."[13] Many of these headaches that thus are lumped together cannot be justifiably classified as types of migraine, and it has never been proved that they are due to abnormalities of blood vessels. The effort to include this motley group of headaches in the migraine category and to imply that they are due to abnormalities of blood vessels is unfortunate and without scientific support.

It is likewise unfortunate that headache due to painful, contracted neck muscles is thought by so many physicians to occur only in emotionally disturbed persons. Muscle contraction and neck pain may occur in all kinds of headaches that have been classified as migraine just as often as they do in "tension headaches."[9, 11, 14] Muscle-contraction headache cannot be considered due to emotional problems in all cases, even though some standard classifications of headache give this impression. Furthermore, headache due to emotional stress is not always associated with painful muscle contraction. The attempt to make a clear-cut distinction between types of headaches, such as common migraine and muscle-contraction headache, and put them into separate categories where no clear distinction exists, accounts for improper treatment of many headache victims. It also has seriously retarded research into causes of headache and attempts to find better treatment for those who have this problem.

Primitive methods for headache treatment.

Some methods used for treatment of headache in the past would not be very popular today. One such treatment is mentioned in an eighth-century Irish manuscript.[15] It consisted of repeating a sequence of words, putting saliva in the palm of the hand, then putting it on the temples and on the back of the head. A cross was then drawn with saliva on the top of the head, after which the letter "U" was drawn in a similar manner. Apparently these acts had to be performed in the correct sequence to be successful. A more aggressive form of therapy was recommended by Albucasis.[2] He suggested treating headaches with a hot iron; and if this was not successful, an incision should be made in the scalp and a piece of garlic inserted in the incision. Some treatments were even more radical.

In South America as well as in some other parts of the world, skulls of primitive man have been found with holes in them. The healing of the bone that has occurred around these skull defects show that many of the original owners of these skulls lived long after the holes were drilled.

Some authorities who have studied these specimens believe that the holes were placed in them in an effort to treat headache and other diseases and some believe that the holes were drilled to allow the evil spirits that caused headache to escape from inside the head.[16] The fact that some skulls have several holes in them suggests that this treatment was not always successful and that it was sometimes repeated (Figure 3). It is almost certain that this therapy was fatal in some cases.

What is placebo effect?

It is possible that all of these primitive treatments for headache appeared to be successful because of what is known today as "placebo effect." This is a term for relief of symptoms that may be obtained from an inactive medicine

HEADACHE—MAN'S MOST COMMON PAIN

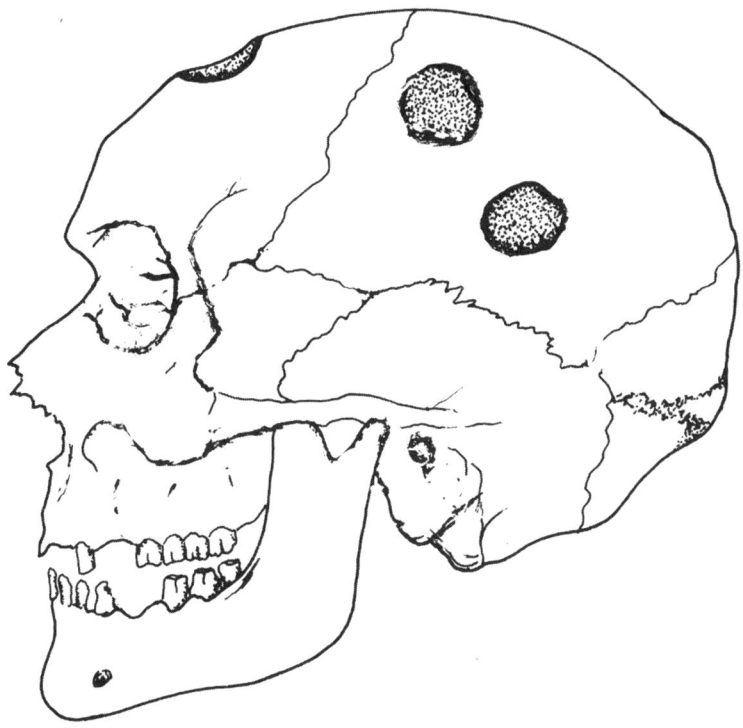

Figure 3. Sketch of a skull with holes in it to illustrate the results of trephination. Placing holes in the skull for treatment of headache and other diseases was widely practiced by ancient man. Skulls showing the effects of trephination have been found in both North and South America as well as in many parts of Europe and Asia. It is reported that trephination for treatment of headache is still practiced in some parts of North Africa as well as in Cuba.

or other type of therapy that produces no healing effect itself, but which is helpful to the patient because of the faith he has in it. This no doubt accounts for at least some of the beneficial effects of folk medicines that have been used in the past. It is also a factor in the apparent success of some types of medicines and treatments that are used today. It has been demonstrated that placebo effect can give relief of pain in one-third of patients.[17] Friedman and Merritt reported in their study of treatment of migraine headache that 25 percent of patients with an acute attack had improvement from a placebo.[18] When several types of commonly used headache medicines were tested along with a placebo to see if they could prevent headache, 50 percent of those individuals receiving an inactive substance reported some improvement. The results reported in their study suggest that the benefit from a placebo was nearly as good as that obtained from drugs commonly used in treatment and prevention of headache. This report can be somewhat misleading, however, since those with only minor improvement were not differentiated from those who obtained complete relief. For this reason this study can give the false impression that good relief of headache resulted from a placebo in half of the patients tested.

Placebo effect in relief of headache is difficult to explain, but it may be partially due to the confidence that comes from learning that no serious disease is present after a physical examination and other tests have been done. It may also be partially accounted for by headaches that resolve spontaneously. There are also several other explanations for placebo effect, but these will not be discussed here.

Headache treatment often not very effective.

Since there are many kinds of headache, there are also many kinds of treatment. In order to treat headache or any other abnormality effectively, its cause should be found and removed if possible. This principle is followed in patients with diseases such as meningitis, brain tumor, or intracranial brain hemorrhage; and these patients usually receive rapid and aggressive therapy. In these cases if the cause of the headache is successfully removed, the symptom of headache usually resolves. This eliminates the need for any ongoing symptomatic treatment.

Management of headache always should be directed toward removal of its cause. This principle is usually not followed in treatment of headache of muscle-contraction and common migraine types. Rather, these headaches are just treated symptomatically with medication. Professional medical personnel who treat patients with common chronic headache often think that these persons are just nervous and they really do not need treatment other than pain killers, tranquilizers, and antidepressants — regardless of how serious the discomfort from the headache may be. The common headache, like the common cold, is often poorly treated by medical personnel. Management consists chiefly of the use of the above named medications for symptomatic relief. These can be helpful in some cases, but they often do not relieve the more severe headaches. More importantly, they do not get rid of the cause of the headache. For immediate treatment of more severe headaches, stronger analgesics as well as narcotics (such as Demerol), tranquilizers and sedatives (such as Valium, Librium, barbiturates), and several other medications are used. These drugs can give good temporary relief, but they carry a risk of drug dependence if used over a long period of time, and in most cases they cannot be considered satisfactory management for persistent or frequently recurring headache. In addition, even though they are relatively safe, they are not entirely without danger. Even over-the-counter analgesics can cause permanent kidney failure or liver damage if they are used in excess.

Other kinds of medication used for treatment of common headache, especially if it has been diagnosed as migraine, include drugs that affect blood vessels. One such drug is propranolol (Inderal). It was learned serendipitously that this drug prevents headache in some people. Even though it affects both the heart and the blood vessels, it is likely that it helps headache by some other as yet unknown mechanism.

Since it has been commonly, but erroneously, believed by most physicians that the majority of common headaches are forms of migraine and that they are caused by dilation of blood vessels, drugs that constrict blood vessels are often used in treating them. The most frequently used blood-vessel-constricting substances are the ergot drugs or combination of ergot with analgesics and other medications. Commonly used preparations include Cafergot, which is a combination of ergot and caffeine, or special preparations of ergot that are placed under the tongue for rapid absorption through the mucous membrane of the mouth. Injectable ergot preparations can be given by intramuscular or intravenous routes. These ergot drugs can be effective in preventing the headache of classic migraine if they are used during the period of warning before the onset of headache, but they are less effective after the headache begins. They are also effective to some extent in many common headaches that are not of the classic migraine type. Some investigators have considered that this is good evidence that these headaches are all due to blood vessel dilation and therefore they too should be called common migraine or migraine without aura. It has been known for years, however, that responsiveness to the ergot drugs does not necessarily parallel the usual criteria for diagnosis of migraine, but rather it correlates better with the severity of the headache.[19] For this reason the response to ergot is not a valid criterion for the diagnosis of migraine, nor is an unfavorable response to ergot preparations and the presence of tight muscles a valid reason to believe that a headache victim is emotionally disturbed. If emotional disturbances were the cause of headaches in persons with tight neck muscles one could expect these persons to get relief of their painful contracted muscles and their headaches by having psychiatric treatment; but psychiatric treatment for headache is usually not successful.

Several kinds of headache therapy depend on physical measures rather than drugs. Biofeedback has been reported to have been beneficial in the hands of some investigators, but as an effective means of headache therapy for large numbers of individuals it has been found to be disappointing[20] as well as quite expensive. Acupuncture has been even less effective. Chiropractic manipulation and hypnosis have been reported to be helpful for some individuals.

The most important principle in treatment of common headache is to find its cause and remove it rather than depending on pain-killing drugs and other symptomatic treatment. It has been demonstrated that most people who have common headache have painful shortening of muscles and fibrous tissue in the neck.[9, 21] The most effective means of treating these headaches is to get rid of the cause by the use of the simple methods described in chapter 2. It has been shown that up to 90 percent of persons with common headaches that are severe enough to cause them to seek medical help can get relief by this simple method.[21, 22] These good results can be obtained in those who do not have one of the life-threatening causes of headache, or any serious emotional disturbance, and who are motivated to follow the instructions.

Although headaches due to brain tumors and other serious diseases make up less than 0.1 percent of all headaches, the possibility that these conditions can be present should be considered in every person with this symptom. In some cases it is difficult to distinguish between common headache and headache due to these serious causes. This differentiation may require examination by a physician; and in some cases x-ray computed tomography (CT) or magnetic resonance imagining (MRI) tests. Because of the urgency in identifying headaches due to serious diseases, some of these serious causes for headaches are described in chapters 5, 6, and 7.

HEADACHE—MAN'S MOST COMMON PAIN

References for Chapter 1.

1. Robey WH. Headache. Philadelphia: JB Lippincott Co, 1931:5.
2. Balyeat RM. Migraine — diagnosis and treatment. Philadelphia: JB Lippincott Co. 1933:2-4.
3. Kunkle EC. Mechanisms of headache. In: Friedman AP, Merritt HH. Headache — diagnosis and treatment. Philadelphia: FA Davis Co, 1963.3.
4. Ziegler DK, Hassanein RS, Couch JR. Characteristics of life headache histories in a nonclinic population. Neurology 1977;27:265-269.
5. Raskin NH, Appenzeller O. Headache. Vol XIX in the series: Major problems in internal medicine. Philadelphia: WB Saunders Co, 1980:1.
6. DiPalma JR. Basic pharmacology in medicine. New York: McGraw-Hill Book Co, 1976:135.
7. Headache Classification Committee of the International Headache Society: Classification and diagnostic criteria for headache disorders, cranial neuralgias and facial pain. Cephalgia 1988;8(Suppl 7):1-96.
8. Ad hoc committee classification of headache, JAMA 1962;6:717.
9. Pozniak-Patewicz E. "Cephalgic" spasm of head and neck muscles. Headache 1976;14:261-266.
10. Raskin NH. Headache. New York: Churchill Livingstone 1988:1.
11. Drummond PD, Lance JW. Clinical Diagnosis and Computer Analysis of Headache Symptoms. J. Neurol Neurosurg Psychiatry 1984;47:128-133.
12. Dalessio DJ. Some current data on headache research. Triangle 1981;20:33-41.
13. Dalessio DJ. Wolff's headache and other head pain. 4th ed. New York: Oxford University Press. 1980:59.
14. Zeigler DK, Hassanein R, Hassanein K. Headache syndromes suggested by factor analysis of symptom variable in a headache prone population. J. Chronic Dis 1971;25:353-363.
15. Friedman AP. The headache, literature and legend. Bull NY Acad Med 1972;48:661-681.
16. Boshes LD. Headache. In: World Book Encyclopedia. Chicago: Field Enterprieses Educatonal Corp, 1960;8:122.
17. Beecher H. The powerful placebo. JAMA 1955;159:1602-1606.
18. Friedman AP, Merritt HH. Treatment of headache. JAMA 1957;163:1111-1117.
19. Barrie MA, Fox WR, Weatherall M, et al. Analysis of symptoms of patients with headaches and their response to treatment with ergot derivatives.

Quart J Med 1968;37:319-336.
20. Raskin NH, Appenzeller O. Headache. Vol XIX in the series: Major problems in internal medicine. Philadelphia: WB Saunders Co, 1980:180.
21. Peterson DI. A simple treatment for chronic headache. Bull Clin Neurosci 1983;48:171-172.
22. Peterson DI. Headache – Modern Concepts of Diagnosis and Management. Prim Care 1984;11:707-721.

2

How to Get Relief from Common Headache

More than 80 percent of persons seeking medical help for treatment of headache are diagnosed as having either migraine without aura or muscle-contraction headache. Many others have headaches caused by head and neck injuries. Unfortunately, those who suffer from these common headaches are often inadequately treated because emphasis is placed on symptomatic drug treatment rather than on measures to get rid of the cause of headache.

Today there is very helpful information for those who suffer from these problems. Most can be successfully treated by simple self-performed therapeutic measures regardless of how long they have suffered from these headaches. The majority of those who have this problem, and even many physicians, do not realize that this is possible. Even many headache specialists believe that persistent and frequently recurring headaches are life-long problems and that nothing effective can be done to get rid of them. They treat this condition by prescribing a succession of drugs which are often of little benefit and which cause undesirable side-effects. Furthermore, some of these drugs will cause drug dependence.

The pessimistic opinion that headache is a lifelong problem is expressed well by Raskin who writes: "Regarding the goals of therapy, it is important for the patient to understand that recurring headache at present cannot be permanently cured."[1] He continues, "The most productive avenue of therapy for chronic tension headache sufferers is the daily use of prophylactic agents." Fortunately for most persons who suffer from headache this is not true. The majority of them can get rid of their headaches in a few weeks or a few months if they carefully and correctly follow the instructions below, giving attention to each detail in order that success can be achieved. In my experience, up to 90 percent of persons are able to obtain relief from headache by this method if neither serious disease nor severe emotional disturbance is present and if litigation or drug dependence is not part of the problem. This is wonderful news for headache sufferers.

The method of treatment for common headache described in the following pages is the most successful presently available. The reasons it is so successful is that it removes the cause of headache rather than depending upon continuous drug use to control symptoms. Finding the underlying cause for this troublesome symptom and removing it is the most important principle in overcoming headache. Lifelong dependence on drugs for symptomatic relief is not good management and should not be resorted to unless the cause cannot be found and eliminated.

This highly successful method of headache treatment will be described in detail, and a simple test to help identify persons most likely to benefit from it will be explained. But first, let us consider some important facts about the structure and function of the neck and how these relate to the cause of headache.

HOW TO GET RELIEF FROM COMMON HEADACHE

Neck mobility and headache.

The head and neck are capable of a wide range of movements which serve several purposes. For example, if we couldn't turn our head our field of vision would be greatly restricted. There would be several other problems. Consider how difficult it would be to communicate with a group of people if we did not have good mobility of our head and neck. It would also be difficult to eat or drink.

This very important mobility of the head and neck is possible because of the elegant design of the joints between the vertebrae and at the junction where the head and neck join. The muscles, tendons, ligaments and other soft tissues provide support for the head and vertebral column, and by their ability to lengthen and shorten they allow normal head and neck movements to occur. There is enough redundancy in this system so that two or three of the intervertebral joints can be fused surgically, as is often done in treating some kinds of neck disease, without significantly decreasing neck mobility.

In spite of its wonderful design, the neck is one of the more structurally weak parts of the body. It is quite susceptible to the effects of stress and injury which often produce protective neck muscle spasm and eventual shortening of the fibrous tissue that holds the muscles and vertebrae in their normal position. This results in a decrease in mobility in the upper part of the neck and at the junction between the head and neck. This abnormality, whether caused by head and neck injury or by stress or other factors, is the most common cause for headache.

There are several causes of neck muscle contraction and

fibrous tissue shortening. Even just being "up tight" from the normal stresses and activities of everyday life may result in neck muscle spasm; and over a period of time this may cause fibrous tissue shortening and decreased range of motion. Head and neck injuries frequently result in neck stiffness. Abnormal positions of the head and neck, especially if prolonged, may produce the same effect. When persistent neck muscle spasm is present, regardless of its cause, decreased range of motion occurs. This happens because the fibrous tissues in the neck become stiff and contracted. This in turn results in neck pain and/or headache. These headaches may continue until the neck muscle spasm and fibrous tissue shortening that cause the decrease of neck mobility are corrected. If normal range of head and neck movement is restored a majority of those who suffer from headache can obtain relief from this painful condition. This is true regardless of whether the headache is due to head and neck injury or if it has been diagnosed as common migraine or muscle-contraction headache and regardless of where the headache is located.

Arthritis of the neck associated with degenerative disease of the discs between the vertebrae is another common cause for headache, especially in the older age group.[2] The chief means by which these headaches are produced is by abnormal fibrous tissue shortening and muscle contraction associated with the neck disease. These headaches can usually be successfully treated by restoring normal range of movement in the area where the head and neck join. This can be accomplished even though no specific therapy is given for the arthritis or degenerative changes in the intervertebral discs. Rarely, some serious disease may be present in the neck which would make any kind of head or neck movement dangerous. These rare diseases include tumor, meningitis, intracranial hemorrhage, blood vessel disease, fractures, dislocations, and conditions that cause instability at the junction where the head and neck join. These conditions will be discussed later in this chapter. If any of these conditions are present they should be treated by a physician.

Test for decrease of neck mobility.

Decreased range of head and neck movement that cause headache can usually be identified by a simple test. The majority of persons with chronic headaches have little or no limitation of forward flexion of the neck or rotation of the neck when performed as isolated movements. For this reason decrease in normal range of motion that is associated with headache may not be discovered by routine physical examinations done by most physicians. There is, however, another kind of head and neck mobility that may be severely restricted in persons with either persistent or frequently recurring headache. This abnormality can be identified by a combination of rotation of the head followed by bending sideways, as illustrated in Figures 1, 2, 3, and 4.

In most persons who do not have frequent or persistent headache, bending sideways after rotation can be accomplished to 15 or 20 degrees without pain or stiffness. However, there may be a considerable variation in the range of this combined movement even in normal individuals. A person with a long, slender neck has greater mobility than one with a short, thick neck. Those in the younger age group have better mobility than individuals beyond the age of forty or fifty years. But most persons with common headache, regardless

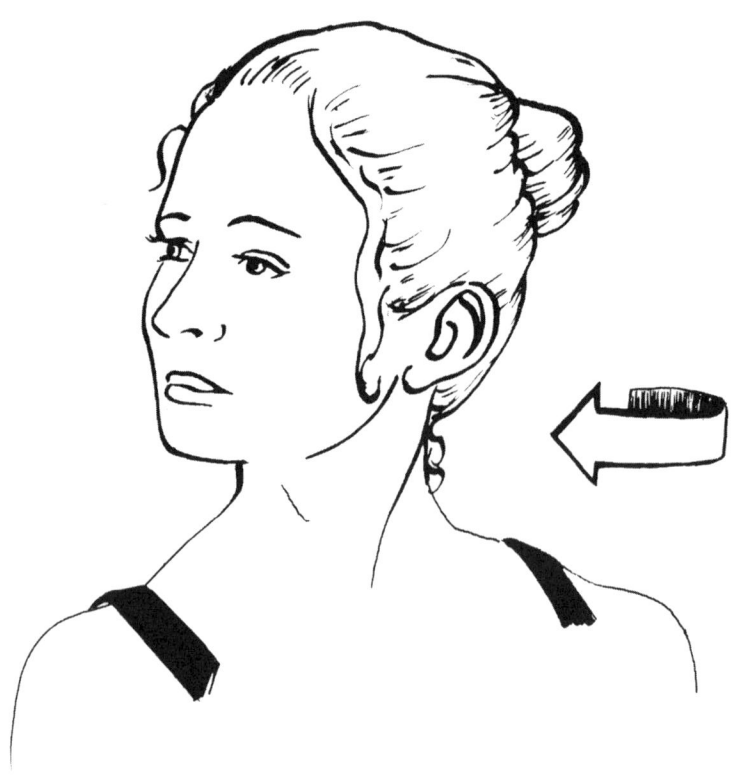

Figure 1. The first step in testing for the presence of abnormal muscle and fibrous tissue contraction associated with common headache and also the first step in the maneuver for treatment of common headache consists of simple rotation of the head through its full range. There should be no tilting of the head and the chin should be kept on the same plane throughout the rotation.

HOW TO GET RELIEF FROM COMMON HEADACHE

Figure 2. The second step in testing for abnormal neck muscle and fibrous tissue contraction and also in treating headache consists of placing the thumb under the jaw holding the head in full rotation by pressing against the jaw and upper teeth with the flexed fingers. Now raise the chin one or two inches.

RELIEF FROM HEADACHE

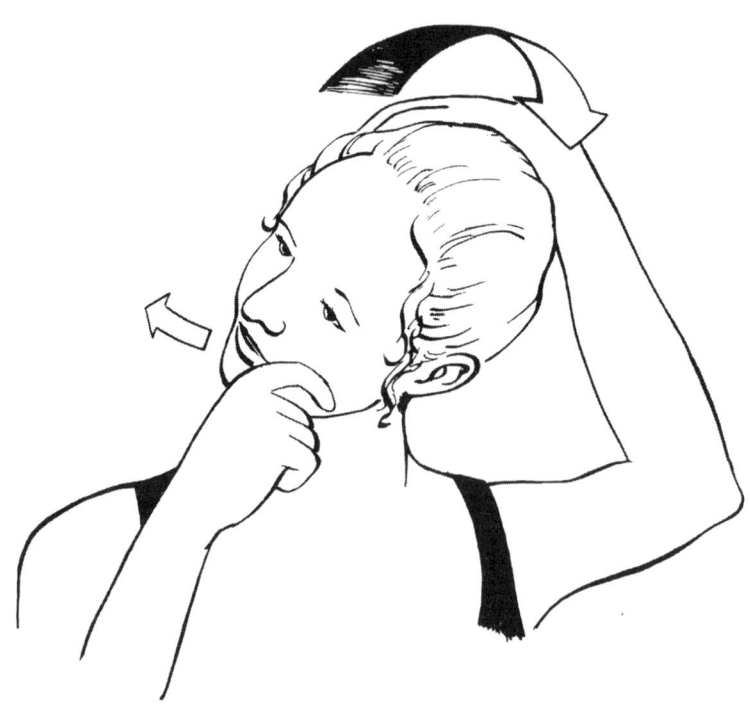

Figure 3 and 4. The third and fourth steps in testing for the presence of contracted neck muscles and fibrous tissue causing headache and the third and fourth steps in the treatment maneuver consists of lateral bending of the fully rotated head and neck. This maneuver should be done slowly and gently and should not cause pain or dizziness. All the lateral bending should be at the top of the neck where the head and neck join. (Read detailed instructions.)

of age or body build or whether they have previously had a diagnosis of migraine or muscle-contraction headache, have severe limitation of this combined movement to much less than 20 degrees. Often the neck is so stiff that no sideways bending is possible when this combination maneuver is attempted even though there may be normal range of motion in performing other kinds of head and neck movements.

Determination of the range of movement by performing combined rotation and sideways (lateral) bending of the head and neck is very helpful in finding the cause of headache. It can be done by the one suffering from headache or by a physician. This test identifies those persons whose headaches are most likely to be relieved by appropriate neck mobilization. The limit of range of motion in this testing maneuver should be the point at which pain begins or dizziness occurs. If these symptoms occur the movement of the head and neck should be decreased slightly until these symptoms are no longer present.

When this examination is performed with the person in a sitting position, the neck should remain as straight as possible in the mid and lower portions. After full rotation of the head and neck to the side, ***all of the lateral bending should occur at the top of the neck***. This is important because it is the muscles and fibrous tissue where the head and neck join that are likely to be painful and abnormally contracted in persons with headache — not those in the lower or middle portions of the neck. When this test is done correctly there is a stretching feeling about two inches behind the ear where the neck muscles are attached to the back of the head. This maneuver to test for the presence of limitation of movement caused by painful, tender muscles and fibrous tissues should be done very slowly and gently; and it should not be continued beyond the point of pain, dizziness, disturbance of vision, or any other discomfort. There should be no jerking movements. The reason for this precaution is that excessive stretching may produce a temporary increase in pain and headache. In addition, if any serious disease of the neck is present it could be made worse by any kind of vigorous or forceful movement that extends beyond the point where pain or dizziness begin.

Correlation between decreased neck mobility and headache.

The importance of having normal range of motion in the area where the head and neck join is not appreciated as it should be. Consequently this common cause for headache is not often recognized. A large number of physicians and even some headache specialists believe that tender, painful, contracted neck muscles and fibrous tissues are the result of headache rather than its cause. Some also falsely believe that only emotionally disturbed persons have tight tender neck muscles. For this reason one of the most common causes of headache is overlooked and not treated successfully by many doctors. Many continue to believe incorrectly that most headaches are caused by instability of control of blood vessels by the brain, and that the pain of most headaches result from blood vessel dilation. For this reason migraine is over-diagnosed. Some physicians even believe that changes in blood vessels are a factor in producing muscle-contraction or myofascial headache. These beliefs account for much of the lack of understanding of the most common cause for headache and for the ineffective treatments and excessive medication used by persons with this problem.

Some headache sufferers have a combination of muscle-contraction headache and migraine. This is often called "combined headache" or "mixed headache." In this condition headache may be due to both dilation of blood vessels and contraction of neck muscles and fibrous tissue. But in the majority of persons with persistent or frequently recurring headache it is unlikely that blood vessel abnormalities are related in any way to the cause of this symptom or the neck muscle and fibrous tissue shortening associated with these headaches.

Medications provide only temporary benefit.

Since there is a strong correlation between headache and restriction of head and neck movement identified by the test described above and illustrated in Figures 1, 2, 3, and 4 it can be predicted that significant relief of headache will result from getting rid of these muscle and fibrous tissue abnormalities. Any measures that can restore normal range of movement and decrease the neck muscle pain and fibrous tissue tightness will prove beneficial. Headache medications including muscle relaxants are seldom effective in accomplishing this important objective.

It is far more important to eliminate the cause of headache than to continue medication for temporary symptomatic relief. Muscle relaxant medication (such as Robaxin, Parafon Forte, Flexeril, and similar drugs) as well as tranquilizers (such as Librium, Valium, Soma, and Ativan) and also other drugs including Inderal provide only temporary relief. Analgesic medicines can be very helpful in relieving headaches symptomatically, but as a means of long-term effective control they are disappointing. In addition, these drugs when given in sufficient dosage to produce adequate pain relief and muscle relaxation may also produce many undesirable side effects including a "drugged feeling." There is also a danger of drug dependency or serious toxic effect when some of these medications are taken over long periods of time. These shortcomings of drug treatment for headache are well known to most headache sufferers but they are often not given sufficient attention by many physicians.

Physical measures and relaxation may be beneficial.

Several types of physical measures may prove helpful in achieving relaxation of neck muscles. These include cervical traction, biofeedback, relaxation therapy, and other measures to be discussed in chapter 3. When controlled studies have been done, however, these methods of treatment have not achieved much success. They may prevent additional muscle and fibrous tissue contraction, but they do not effectively overcome that which is already present.

A simple effective treatment for chronic headache.

There is a simple, effective method of neck muscle and fibrous tissue stretching that can restore normal mobility where the head and neck join and give relief to around 90 percent of those suffering from chronic or frequently recurring headache. This method gets rid of the cause of most headaches. It has been developed and used over a period of many years with a high rate of success in patients who have failed to get relief of headache from other kinds of treatment. Its objective is to restore normal range of motion in the area where the head and neck join. This program of therapy employs the same sequence of simple maneuvers illustrated in Figures 1, 2, 3, and 4 that are also used in testing. This simple method of headache treatment is usually successful for anyone who has limitation of combined rotation and lateral bending of the head and neck of less than 15 or 20 degrees when tested in the manner described above and if the headache is not due to serious disease or severe emotional disturbance or associated with drug dependence.

Headache is the most common myofacial pain syndrome. The most effective method of treatment is to get rid of its cause by correctly and persistently stretching the neck muscles and fibrous tissue where the head and neck join to restore normal range of motion in this area.

The neck muscle and fibrous tissue mobilization treatment for headache is done in the following manner. The four steps are done in sequence as a single stretching maneuver; they are not four separate stretching exercises. They must be done exactly as described below to be effective.

Step 1: Rotate the head to one side as far as possible without producing discomfort. The chin should be kept at the same level on a horizontal plane throughout the entire rotation. There should be no tilting of the head or any movement of the head or neck other than simple rotation as illustrated in Figure 1. Now raise the chin one or two inches. Do not move the shoulders or rotate the body. Hold the head in this position while doing Step 2.

If there is tenderness just below the horizontal bony ridge in the back part of the head, massage this area firmly with the fingertips prior to doing Step 1.

Step 2: The hand on the side of the body toward which the head is turned is now placed against the side of the chin and the upper teeth in such a manner that it can reinforce Step 1. This is done by placing the thumb under the chin with the flexed index finger against the side of the chin and upper jaw to assist the rotation performed in Step 1. The muscles of the neck are then relaxed so the hand is doing all the work of rotating the head as illustrated in Figure 2. If this stretching maneuver causes pain in the lower jaw or if temporomandibular joint disease (TMJ syndrome) is present the side of the flexed pointer finger should exert pressure against the upper teeth only so there is no pressure on the lower jaw or stress on the temporomandibular (TM) joint.

Step 3: The other hand is then placed directly over the top of the head until the middle finger touches the top of the ear on the opposite side of the head, as illustrated in Figures 3 and 4. The elbow of the arm that is over the head should be in line with an imaginary line passing through both ears.

Step 4: Gentle pressure is now exerted by the hand that is pushing against the chin and upper jaw to keep the head rotated and the chin slightly elevated. While this is done the other hand that is touching the ear should gently pull the head sideways as if to roll it off the top of the neck. This combined movement of the two hands produces a rotary effect at the junction between the head and neck. There should be no movement or lateral bending in the midportion or the lower portion of the neck. All the movement and stretching should occur where the head and neck join. This maneuver should be done slowly and gently to avoid pain. There should be no quick or jerking movements.

HOW TO GET RELIEF FROM COMMON HEADACHE

Hold the head in this position of rotation and sideways bending for ten seconds. Then perform the same four steps in the opposite direction in a similar manner for another ten seconds. Then repeat this total sequence three times for a total of sixty seconds of stretching. **<u>There should be a feeling of stretching in the area where the head and neck join</u>**. This is important. The stretching feeling should be felt about two inches behind the ear on either side. This maneuver should be done frequently for best results. It should be done to each side **<u>at least</u>** three or four times every hour initially and later three to four times daily until normal range of motion is achieved. This is accomplished by gradually stretching a fraction of an inch more each time the maneuver is done. **<u>Relief from headache will closely parallel the amount of normal mobility that is attained.</u>** Achieving normal range of motion where the head and neck join is the most important goal to be accomplished in eliminating the cause of common headache.

In order to perform Steps 1, 2, 3, and 4 correctly, there are several important principles to keep in mind. These are discussed now in greater detail and with some repetition of the most important points in order that the stretching sequence will be performed correctly. The common mistakes in doing this maneuver that I have observed being made by those who are not successful in overcoming headache are pointed out.

1. The lower portion of the neck and the middle part of the neck should be kept as straight as possible. All of the movement of lateral bending produced by the hand that is touching the ear as it gently rolls the head sideways should occur in the upper part of the neck. In this way the tight, contracted muscles and fibrous tissue that decrease mobility in

this area are gently stretched without pain or dizziness. ***If the lateral (sideways) bending movement occurs at the bottom of the neck, the stretching is ineffective for relief of headache.*** Failure to keep the neck straight and incorrectly bending from the lower or midportion of the neck rather than from the upper part of the neck where the head and neck join is the most common mistake that is made when performing this therapeutic stretching maneuver.

    2. When the four steps of the gentle stretching maneuver are performed in sequence the body and shoulders should remain stationary without any rotation of the shoulders. The entire maneuver consists of two simple movements: rotation of the head and neck in the first and second steps, and lateral bending in the area where the head and neck join in the third and fourth steps. In order to achieve adequate mobility it is ***essential*** to feel stretching and pulling of the muscles in the back of the head where the neck muscles attach to the head between the ear and the midline of the back of the head. ***If stretching is not felt in this area the maneuver is not being done correctly.*** Some persons may have to tilt the head back further by raising the chin another inch to produce this stretching feeling, while a few individuals may have to lower the chin to or slightly below a horizontal plane to produce this feeling of stretching.

    3. Another common cause for failure to obtain relief from headache by this method is that of not performing the neck mobilization frequently enough. ***It is essential to do it frequently.*** Most people forget unless they have something to remind them to do it. When watching TV do it every time a commercial comes on. If there is a chime clock in the house do it every time the chime sounds. A watch that can sound

an alarm at predetermined intervals of less than one hour is equally good. When reading a book or magazine do the maneuver after reading every five or six pages. The more frequently it is done, the better; but do not stretch too hard because this is counterproductive. If done too vigorously this maneuver may produce pain or headache and may cause a temporary increase in tightness of the neck muscles.

4. Progress in neck mobilization to achieve normal range of motion can be monitored by estimating the degrees of lateral (sideways) bending that is accomplished when performing the sequence of maneuvers illustrated in Figures 3 and 4 and described in Step 4. If the mobilization maneuver is done correctly relief from headache correlates closely with success in achieving normal range of movement. Those who do the neck mobilization program frequently and correctly usually accomplish this in a few weeks to a few months. Those who do not follow the instructions correctly continue to have restricted range of motion and poor relief from headache. Nearly all who fail to obtain relief from headache by this method are found on examination to still have severe limitation of movement when they are tested for head and neck mobility. This shows that they have not performed the stretching maneuver correctly or frequently enough.

Around ten percent of people report that the stretching maneuver causes headache or makes their headaches worse. This demonstrates with near 100 percent likelihood that these headaches originate in tissues where the head and neck join. These persons should do the maneuver very gently and only three or four times a day initially. If they continue doing the four-step stretching maneuver correctly, nearly all of them will have less headaches in three to four weeks and most of them will have resolution of their headaches within two to three months if they achieve normal range of motion where the head and neck join.

A common cause for failure in any kind of treatment program is non-compliance. This also has been true of the neck mobilization method for treatment of headache. However, it is easy to determine if the stretching maneuver is being done correctly. Neck mobility can be tested as described and illustrated in Figures 1, 2, 3, and 4. If the stretching has been done properly so normal or near normal range of motion has been accomplished, headache will usually be gone or greatly decreased. There have been cases in which patients insisted that they were doing the stretching maneuver frequently and correctly, but when asked to demonstrate how they performed it they did not know how to do it. In other cases family members have revealed that they have never observed the patient performing the stretching maneuvers. Failure to follow instructions accounts for most of the failures of this method of headache treatment.

5. The arm that pulls the head to bend it sideways as shown in Figures 3 and 4 should be directed straight over the top of the head toward the ear, and not around the back of the head.

6. After the maneuver has been performed for ten seconds in one direction, the same sequence of four steps should be done for ten seconds in the opposite direction. In this case the position of the hands is reversed, always using the hand on the side to which the chin is turned for pressure against the jaw. The opposite hand is then placed across the top of the head to touch the top of the ear. If the hands are placed in any other position the maneuver cannot be done correctly.

7. This series of gentle stretching movements should be performed frequently throughout the day for at least four to eight weeks, or until the headaches are relieved and normal range of motion achieved. After the headaches have been relieved, one series of stretching maneuvers done three or four times daily is usually sufficient to keep the muscles and fibrous tissues at their normal length. ***Do not discontinue the stretching.*** If it is discontinued the neck muscles may get tight again and the headaches may reoccur after a few months.

8. Some individuals, and especially those with severely contracted neck muscles and fibrous tissue, may experience some increase in tenderness in the upper portion of the neck and the base of the skull, and even some radiation of pain to the top of the head after the first few stretching maneuvers. This is one of the reasons why very gentle stretching should be done initially. If vigorous stretching is done, pain and headache may be increased and overstretching may even precipitate an attack of headache. A few people will experience some increase in headache initially even if they exercise very gently, but nevertheless, it is essential to achieve normal range of motion to get relief from headache. ***Relief from headache closely parallels the degree of normal range of motion that is achieved.*** Application of heat over the neck muscles before performing the neck muscle stretching maneuver will decrease neck muscle pain. This can be accomplished by getting into a hot shower and allowing hot water to spray on the neck, by getting into a hot tub or Jacuzzi, or even by holding a hot wash cloth on the neck. If the neck remains stiff with poor mobility, headaches are likely to continue. If the neck mobilization maneuver is done correctly there is a success rate of up

to 90 percent. Noncompliance is the chief cause of failure.

9. The objective of the stretching exercise is to gradually increase the range of motion of rotation and lateral bending of the head at its junction with the neck. When a range of 15 to 20 degrees in lateral bending is accomplished in each direction most persons with headache experience major improvement and often they have complete relief from this symptom. If the stretching maneuver is done frequently and correctly, some individuals obtain relief within a few days, but others may experience slow relief over a period of several weeks. Those individuals who have had severe headaches for many years may need to do the stretching exercises for an even longer period of time — even several months — before adequate mobilization is achieved.

10. Although the neck stretching maneuver illustrated in Figures 1, 2, 3, and 4 is primarily for prevention of common headache, it can in some cases abort an acute attack of headache if performed as soon as the headache begins.

This neck mobilization maneuver is very simple but it must be done correctly. Very few people do it correctly unless they carefully observe the illustrations and read the instructions several times. Those individuals who do not get relief from headache by this method in two to three months may have a kind of headache other than muscle-contraction (or myofascial) headache or "common migraine," but it is much more likely that they have not done the mobilization maneuver correctly or frequently enough. One of the variants of "Murphy's Law" says that "anything that can be done wrong will be done wrong." That has been true of the neck mobilization maneuver described above. This stretching maneuver must be done exactly as illustrated to be effective. Other kinds of neck stretching traditionally recommended by physical therapists and physicians have been demonstrated to be poorly effective for relief of headache.

The following list consists of a review of the most common reasons for failure to achieve neck mobility and obtain relief from headache:

1. Bending from the midportion or bottom of the neck rather than the area where the head and neck join.

2. Trying to do the four steps all at once instead of doing them in sequence and thus not doing any of them right. Do one step at a time with emphasis on doing each step correctly.

3. Not doing the maneuver frequently enough. If a person is trying to loosen a stiff joint he will stretch it many times a day. The neck mobilization maneuver must also be done many times a day to achieve best results.

4. Stopping the program of neck stretching after a few days or weeks before normal range of motion has been achieved. Noncompliance with instructions is the most common cause for failure to get rid of headache by this method.

A follow-up study of sixty persons who were instructed about how to do the stretching maneuver was done three months to one year after they started the program. There had been poor compliance. Forty percent of these persons had not done the stretching frequently enough. Even some of these had at least partial relief from headache.

5. Some persons have said they could not do the mobilization maneuver because "it hurts." This usually happens because they are jerking the head like a chiropractic manipulation or they are stretching too hard.

6. Even some physicians don't teach or perform the maneuver correctly because they believe "one kind of neck

stretching is like any other kind of neck stretching." They still continue to do the old ineffective lateral stretching and yoga type rotational exercises which have been used unsuccessfully in treatment of headache for many years.

7. Some say, "It doesn't make sense" to try to get rid of headaches by neck mobilization because they believe incorrectly that most headaches are due to abnormalities inside the head. For this reason some fail to do the stretching and miss a golden opportunity to get rid of headache.

8. Some individuals are not successful because they would rather keep on taking drugs for temporary relief than take the time and make the effort needed to get rid of the cause of headache. Some of these individuals are addicted to medication. Drug dependent persons are often poorly motivated to get rid of their headaches because their chief interest and objective is to obtain drugs. Some of these persons may have to go through a drug rehabilitation program to get off these medications.

9. Some persons who have had severe headaches for many years or who are incapacitated by headache think this method of headache treatment is just **too simple to help them**. But if they learn to do the neck mobilization maneuver correctly and by this means lengthen their shortened neck muscles and fibrous tissue so normal range of motion is achieved most of them will get over their headaches regardless of how long they have had them. I have often asked persons who have gotten relief from headache by this means if they had initially thought it was too simple to help them. Many of them have answered: "Yes, I doubted that such a simple thing could get rid of my severe headaches. but I did it because I had tried all the other treatments without success. I still had

headaches and I knew of nothing else that offered hope."

10. Many persons have severe headaches following head and neck injuries from motor vehicle accidents and from industrial injuries. Some of these persons who are involved in litigation are poorly motivated to get rid of their headaches and other symptoms. They would prefer to be treated by the "green poultice" of a large financial settlement from the insurance company. As a neurologist I have examined some of these persons. They often manifest false abnormalities when the neurological examination is being performed in an effort to strengthen their case. Most persons with headache and neck pain after motor vehicle accidents get good relief from these symptoms by correctly performing the neck mobilization program to accomplish normal range of motion where the head and neck join.

11. Persons with serious emotional problems may need help in resolving these problems. Psychiatric treatment often helps these persons with their emotional disturbances but psychiatric counseling as a treatment for headache has a very low success rate.

There are several wrong ways to do neck mobilization.

There are other ways in which the rotation and lateral bending exercise can be done but they are not satisfactory. One variant of this maneuver can be done by first flexing the head and neck forward and then rotating the head, moving the chin toward one shoulder. When the maneuver is done in this manner, it is difficult to keep the lower part of the neck straight and therefore difficult to estimate the degrees of limitation of neck movement.

A similar stretching exercise can be done by performing lateral bending before rotation, but this is more difficult and stretching is less effective because it is difficult to use the hands to assist neck stretching when done in this way. Simple lateral bending without initial rotation does not stretch muscles in the right place and is not very beneficial in treating headache. Billig[3] described a neck-stretching exercise consisting of rotation and lateral bending to stretch the muscles in the middle and lower portions of the cervical area for treatment of neck pain. In my experience this exercise is not helpful for headache relief because it does not stretch the muscles and fibrous tissue in the right place.

After the correct method of neck stretching for relief from headache has been learned, this maneuver can be done without assistance from the hands by simply moving the head and neck to the appropriate positions of rotations and lateral bending similar to those illustrated in Figures 1, 2, 3, and 4. The maneuver can be done in this manner when a person is in any place or situation in which performing it with assistance from the hands would not be feasible such as in the office, a restaurant, a theater, church, or other public place. It is essential, however, to perform the maneuver in such a manner that it causes a stretching feeling between the ear and midline of the back of the head where the neck muscles attach to the head.

Not like chiropractic manipulation.

The neck mobilization maneuver for relief from headache is entirely different from chiropractic manipulation.

Chiropractic manipulation usually consists of jerking movements intended to snap the neck and put vertebrae that are "out of place" — "back in place." The neck mobilization maneuver for relief from headache is different. It is done very slowly and gently to stretch abnormally contracted neck muscles and fibrous tissue so normal range of motion can be achieved. There should be no jerking or quick forceful movements. There are other important differences. Chiropractic manipulations are done by a therapist. If they provide relief it is usually only temporary. They cannot be done frequently enough and they are expensive. The neck mobilization maneuver is done by the person who suffers from headache rather than by a therapist. It should be done several times each hour until normal range of movement has been achieved. It can give lasting benefit if done correctly and it costs nothing.

Research study to compare neck stretching techniques.

A research study was designed to compare the results obtained in treatment of headache by the above described combined rotation and lateral bending neck mobilization exercises as shown in Figures 1, 2, 3, and 4 with those obtained from a standard neck-stretching program.[4, 5] This standard neck-stretching method consists of simple lateral bending and forward bending of the neck and the "yoga" type head and neck rotation exercise. These exercises have been recommended for many years by physical therapists and physicians for neck muscle stretching. They have proven of little benefit for treatment of headache. This study demonstrated the much greater effectiveness of the combination rotation and lateral flexion stretching exercise described in Steps 1, 2, 3, and 4 than traditional neck exercises. The results are given in Table 1 and summarized in the following four paragraphs.

There were ten persons in each group, and each followed his respective neck-stretching exercise program for two months. Half of those who performed the above described combined rotation and lateral bending stretching program (illustrated in Figures 1, 2, 3, and 4) obtained complete or near-complete relief of their headache. Another four of the members of this group experienced 60-70 percent relief. One had 30-60 percent relief. (This individual was still not doing the exercises correctly after three sessions of instruction and it was later learned that she was drug dependent. Had this been known she would not have been included in the study.)

Of those who did the traditional neck care exercise program of simple lateral bending and "yoga" type head and neck rotation, only one person had complete relief.* Five felt no improvement. One had 60-90 percent relief, and three had 10-30 percent relief.

Several types of persons with headache were not included in this study. Those not included were 1) those who appeared to be drug dependent, 2) those who were severely depressed, or who had other kinds of serious emotional problems, 3) those who had some serious neurological disease, and 4) those who

---

*This person reported by telephone that she got relief from headache after two months but she did not return for examination. Later she revealed that she did not have confidence in the neck mobilization program so she went elsewhere for a course of biofeedback. She got no relief from this. Several months later she returned to learn how to do the effective kind of neck mobilization. When she did the effective neck-stretching program she got relief from headache.

were involved in litigation regarding personal injury.

After the comparative study of the two groups was completed, the control group that initially had done the less effective traditional neck exercises then did the effective neck-stretching program during a second two-month period. All but one of these also experienced relief from headache. (This patient was having domestic problems that later led to divorce. She did not give this information when she entered the headache study.) Although this is the first controlled study of this method of treatment for common headache, it has been used for a period of nearly twenty years in successfully treating several thousand headache patients.

Additional measures that may help relieve chronic headache.

Several other measures, although of secondary importance, may prove helpful for some persons in the overall treatment of common headache. These include the following:

1. Some individuals may need to continue medication for relief of headache for a few weeks during the neck-stretching program until normal range of motion is achieved. These medications may include Inderal (which helps a few people), codeine, Darvon, or similar drugs for symptomatic relief of pain. Antidepressants (such as Elavil) and tranquilizers (such as Valium and Librium) or other medications that have been helpful in relieving headache may need to be continued until normal mobility has been achieved. Other medications which may provide temporary benefit include Naprosyn, Motrin, aspirin, and other nonsteroidal anti-inflammatory drugs, and calcium channel blockers such as verapamil, nifedipine, and

Table 1.

Comparison of results obtained by two groups of persons with chronic headache who performed two different types of neck muscle stretching exercises. The difference between results obtained by the study group and the control group are statistically significant ($p < 0.01$).

Group and type of treatment	Number in group	Relief from headache obtained in two months				
		None	Less than 30%	30-60%	60-90%	Greater than 90%
Study Group I. Rotation and lateral flexion (first two month period)	10	—	—	1	4	5
Control Group II. Lateral flexion and "yoga" type rotation of the head and neck (first two month period)	10	4	3	1	1	1
Control Group III. Rotation and lateral flexion (second two month period)*	9**	1	1	1	4	2

*After the first two month period the control group performed the effective neck stretching program and then they also got good relief from headache. The difference between results obtained by this group on the two different neck stretching programs is statistically significant ($p < 0.05$).

**The person from the control group that got greater than 90% improvement is not included in this group.

nimodipine. Newer drugs called triptans can be very effective for symptomatic relief. These triptans including Imitrex, Zomig, and Maxalt can be used for acute headache attacks if needed. After normal range of motion is achieved these medications will usually not be necessary.

2. A neck collar to support the head in a neutral position may prove beneficial for some persons. This is especially true if headaches are increased by positional factors such as forward flexion of the neck that occurs when ironing, vacuuming, or doing many other kinds of everyday activities. The neck collar should not be worn continuously because if this is done the neck muscles may become weak. Individuals who awaken with headache during the night or in the morning are often greatly helped by use of a neck collar while they sleep at night. The collar should support the head and neck in a neutral or slightly flexed position. In my experience, a neck collar is usually superior to various kinds of cervical pillows because most cervical pillows provide good support only while the person is lying on his back. The neck collar should never hyperextend the head and neck because this may make headache worse. It is often better to wear the neck collar backward than in the usual manner so it will not elevate the chin and bend the neck back. The neck collar should provide support with the neck bent slightly forward so the neck muscles will relax.

3. Relaxation programs often prove to be beneficial. There are several techniques for learning relaxation. Some of these techniques involve use of tape recordings that assist in achieving this goal. A simple relaxation program can be accomplished by lying down for a period of three to five minutes several times a day. During this time complete mental and physical relaxation should be achieved. One may fanta-

size floating on a cloud, floating in a tropical lagoon, or being in some other quiet and restful environment. An attempt should be made to eliminate all emotions of worry, anxiety, and anger. Each part of the body should be relaxed in sequence — including the toes, the feet, the legs, thighs, hands, arms, neck, and the entire body. Breathing should be slow. the eyes should be closed and the mouth should be open, with the jaw relaxed. This type of therapy can be beneficial for relaxation of muscle tension in all parts of the body. Relaxation therapy can help prevent additional muscle spasm but it cannot stretch fibrous tissue that is already shortened. Only the mobilization maneuver illustrated in Figures 1, 2, 3, and 4 can do this effectively.[5]

4. For those who do not obtain adequate physical exercise, a good exercise program may be necessary in order to achieve muscle relaxation. This can consist of calisthenics — especially stretching exercises for all muscle groups all over the body. Special attention should be given to the muscles of the back. Some type of sports activity (such as tennis or golf) can also be very beneficial. Other physical activity may include running, walking, or swimming. Exercise should be performed to the point of mild fatigue so subsequent muscle relaxation occurs. It has been reported that some persons get good relief from chronic headache by jogging regularly even if they use no specific headache treatment. The likely reason for this is that muscle relaxation results from the physical exercise obtained by jogging. However, a few individuals — especially those with arthritis or some other disease of the neck — may experience an increase in headache from jarring of the neck associated with running or jogging. After normal range of head and neck movement has been achieved, jogging or running can usually be done without causing headache.

HOW TO GET RELIEF FROM COMMON HEADACHE

Exercise that is enjoyable is much more beneficial than activity that is unpleasant or that seems a drudgery.

5. Good posture is of importance in relieving muscle tension. The head and neck should be held up with the neck straight and not bent forward. If one stands as tall as possible, this objective is usually achieved. One method of testing for proper posture is to stand with the back against a wall, with heels, buttocks, shoulders, and head touching the wall. Standing and sitting in proper positions can lesson tension on muscles that maintain posture, including those in the neck.

6. In treatment of migraine, emphasis is placed upon the importance of change in lifestyle. This includes change of thought patterns in an attempt to overcome feelings of anger, guilt, hostility, resentment, anxiety, and frustration. Practice of general good health measures such as getting adequate rest and exercise, eating healthful foods, and eliminating the use of alcohol and caffeine containing beverages are often beneficial. These factors may be helpful for persons with all kinds of headaches whether they have been classified as migraine or tension headache. St. Francis' "Prayer of Serenity" can assist in achieving a healthy mental attitude: "God grant me the serenity to accept the things I cannot change, courage to change the things I can, and the wisdom to know the difference." If a person's work situation and/or living conditions are intolerably stressful, changes in these circumstances may be necessary.

"Laugh therapy" recommended by Norman Cousins for some other kinds of chronic pain may also be helpful.[6, 7] This can consist of reading several jokes each day or watching sitcoms that induce laughter. This approach to treatment of headache pain is usually ineffective by itself because normal range of head and neck movement must also be achieved.

7. Headaches in some individuals are precipitated or aggravated by inadequate fluid intake resulting in a state of chronic dehydration. This is especially true in unusually hot weather. All individuals with headache should drink an adequate amount of water. A good program for adequate fluid intake in normal situations and average environmental temperatures consists of drinking two glasses of water on arising in the morning before dressing or eating breakfast. Then drink at last two more glasses of water by ten o'clock, and at least another two glasses by two o'clock. This amount of water should be in addition to regularly used fluids such as milk, juice, and coffee. Changes in environmental surroundings and increases of temperatures may greatly change fluid intake requirements.

8. Eliminating foods or beverages that cause headache may be helpful for some people (see chapter 9).

9. Application of heat and massage to the shoulders and neck may be of assistance in decreasing pain and muscle spasm. A hot towel applied to the neck for a few minutes will make the neck mobilization maneuver easier to perform without causing pain.

Some conditions make any kind of head and neck movement dangerous.

When the test for the presence of painful, contracted neck muscle and fibrous tissue is performed or when therapeutic stretching is done it should be recognized that there are some conditions which may be aggravated by neck stretching or any other kind of head or neck movement. For example, if a severe headache of recent onset is present, it is possible that it could be caused by meningitis, tumor, intracranial hemorrhage, stroke, or undiagnosed injury (such as fracture or dislocation of the neck). Some of these conditions could be aggravated by any kind of movement of the head or neck. All of these conditions are rare and are usually associated with other abnormalities. It is unlikely that they would be confused with migraine or muscle-contraction headache.

Neck stretching or neck movement of any type should not be done if there is a tumor in the neck. There are several types of malignant tumors that tend to spread from their site of origin to bone, including the skull and the vertebrae of the neck. Tumors that tend to metastasize to bone include those that develop in lung, prostate, breast, kidney, and thyroid gland; but any kind of malignant tumor can on some occasions spread to neck structures. Sometimes these tumors may produce neck pain and headache before they can be identified by x-ray examination, although this is very uncommon.

Several other rare conditions may make any kind of vigorous movement of the neck hazardous. One of these abnormalities consists of a congenital instability of the joints between the head and the neck due to failure of formation of some of the bone and fibrous tissue in this region. Individuals with this abnormality may have injury to the spinal cord from any kind of vigorous head and neck movement. This kind of injury occasionally occurs during chiropractic manipulation. Some individuals with this abnormality have even become paralyzed from very minor injuries such as falling, especially if the fall caused the head and neck to be bent backward. This kind of instability of the junction area between the head and neck is very rare, but if present it is even dangerous to participate in sports. Patients with rheumatoid arthritis often develop bone destruction in the upper portion of the cervical spine and have an acquired instability in which the same danger is present. Even minor falls or sudden hyperextension of the neck in these persons have been known to produce irreversible spinal cord damage.

Vigorous neck movement can occasionally cause damage to blood vessels in this region. Blood is supplied to the brain through four main blood vessels. These vessels consist of two carotid arteries and two vertebral arteries. The vertebral arteries in their normal course from the upper portion of the chest to the brain pass through some holes in the sides of the cervical vertebrae where they are relatively well protected. As they leave the neck and go into the head, there is some redundancy to allow for movement of the head and neck without danger of stretching or compressing these arteries. However, it has been demonstrated that in some individuals complete rotation of the head and neck to one side, especially if this is done when the head and neck are bent backward, may cause transient blocking of one of these blood vessels. If both vessels are normal, temporary occlusion of one vessel usually causes no abnormality; but if one of these blood vessels is already occluded by arteriosclerosis or a blood clot, compression of the second vessel may cause loss of blood supply to the brain stem. If this type of abnormality is present there have been occasional cases in which either chiropractic manipulation or vigorous turning of the head to look to one side have caused a stroke from compression or injury to a diseased vertebral artery. The same thing has occurred occasionally even in young persons with normal blood vessels who have had severe hyperextension neck injuries as may happen in some types of football injuries or in automobile accidents. It is remotely possible that any kind of movement of the head and neck could compress or injure blood vessels in an occasional person. but it is very unlikely that rotation and lateral bending, as described in this chapter, would cause blood vessel injury or any other harm to anyone if the maneuver is done gently and according to instructions, stopping short of pain or dizziness.

Even though it is likely that less than one in 10,000 persons have any type of preexisting abnormality that could be made worse in any way by head and neck turning, as described above, this danger may exist in a few cases. If there is any possibility of these conditions being present, care should be taken in performing any kind of head and neck movements or participating in sports. If pain other than muscle pain occurs, or if severe dizziness is present when the testing maneuver is done or while stretching contracted neck muscles, a physician should be consulted to see if some serious abnormality is present.

Summary and conclusions.

There are many causes for headache. These may include emotional problems such as anxiety, anger, worry, tension, frustration, and depression. These emotions, however, are common to most people whether or not they have headache. So obviously these emotions alone do not necessarily cause headache. Head and neck injury does not correlate very well with the frequency, duration, and severity of headache. Other abnormalities such as arthritis of the cervical spine, herniated discs in the cervical area, or neck muscle strain may also result in headache. The common denominator of these conditions is abnormally contracted neck muscles and fibrous tissue. This

RELIEF FROM HEADACHE

is the most common cause of headache regardless of what produces the neck muscle and fibrous tissue abnormality.

These abnormal conditions of neck muscles and fibrous tissue are poorly combatted by most kinds of headache treatments because most headache treatments do not get rid of this common cause for headache. If none of the serious head or neck injuries or diseases previously mentioned are present, relief can be obtained in most cases by the simple neck mobilization and exercise maneuver illustrated in Figures 1, 2, 3, and 4 with assistance in some cases from secondary measures which are also described in this chapter.

The most important principle to follow in treatment of headache is to get rid of its cause. In most cases this can be successfully accomplished by achieving normal range of motion in the upper part of the neck and at the junction where the head and neck join. Relief from headache will usually closely parallel the amount of normal range of motion that is achieved in this area. In occasional cases it may be necessary to obtain treatment for specific diseases of the head or neck. These include such conditions as herniated intervertebral disc, arthritis, infection, tumors, or other abnormalities mentioned above.

References for Chapter 2.

1. Raskin NH. Headache. 2nd ed. New York: Churchill Livingstone, 1988:220-222.
2. Brain DM. Some unsolved problems of cervical spondylosis. BMJ 1963;1:771-777.
3. Billig HE. The release of fascial ligamentous contractures in physical rehabilitation. Industrial Medicine 1945;14:270-273.
4. Peterson DI. A simple treatment for chronic headache. Bull Clin Neurosci 1983;48:171-172.
5. Peterson DI. Headache — modern concepts of diagnosis and management. Prim Care 1984;11:707-721.
6. Cousins N. Anatomy of an illness (as perceived by the patient). N Engl J Med 1976;295:1458-1463.
7. Cousins N. Anatomy of an illness. Readers Digest (June) 1977;110:130-134.

3

Muscle Spasm in the Neck and Scalp Can Cause Headache

What is muscle-contraction headache?

Muscle-contraction or myofascial headache is the most frequently occurring kind of headache, and most people have suffered from it at one time or another. The term "tension headache" is usually considered to be synonymous with muscle-contraction headache, and many physicians consider "psychogenic headache" to be another synonym for this condition. In its most characteristic form it is often considered to be a sensation of aching and pressure which can be located anywhere in the head. It frequently consists of a band-like feeling around the head associated with pain and tightness of the neck muscles. The headache may last for variable periods of time; and it may be continuous for days, weeks, months, or even years. Some believe there is no warning prior to the headache attack. Traditionally it is believed that the only associated symptoms are nervousness, anxiety, depression, and painful contraction of the neck and scalp muscles. The headache is considered by many to be nonthrobbing in type.

Many of these traditional views of muscle-contraction or tension headache are incorrect. For example, better observers have found that nearly 50 percent of patients with muscle-contraction headache have throbbing-type headache on some occasions. Half of them have associated visual disturbances which are similar to those seen in migraine without aura, but they are usually less dramatic than those experienced with migraine with aura. Studies of patients with headache have also shown that one-third of patients with muscle-contraction headache have nausea and/or vomiting on at least some occasions, especially when the headache is severe. As the characteristics of muscle-contraction headache are studied more carefully, the difference between it and migraine without aura becomes indistinct. Both kinds of headache can be precipitated by nervousness and emotional disturbances. Both of them are associated with pain, tenderness, and tightness of the neck muscles. And either can be unilateral or bilateral. Either kind of headache may be throbbing in type on some occasions and nonthrobbing on other occasions. Either one can be associated with visual disturbances, and the same kinds of treatment can be effective in relieving either headache. Furthermore, electrical tests demonstrate as much neck muscle-contraction in patients with migraine as in those with tension headache.[1, 2]

In the past many authorities who treat headache have made a clear distinction between muscle-contraction headache and migraine without aura. They have considered them to be two entirely different kinds of condition. Muscle-

MUSCLE SPASM IN THE NECK AND SCALP

contraction headache was said to be due to nervousness, anxiety, and other emotional disturbances, and associated with tight neck muscles. Common migraine was thought to be due to instability of control of blood vessels by the nervous system, resulting in painful dilation of the blood vessels of the head (chiefly of the scalp).

The classification of headache on page 10 suggests that common migraine and muscle-contraction headache are entirely different entities. It is becoming more apparent, however, that the difference between them is somewhat nebulous. Raskin and Appenzeller state, "There is no compelling evidence to support a biological mechan(ism) of tension headache that is qualitatively different from that of migraine."[3] Ziegler, who is an authority on the causes of headaches, states, "…the distinction between common migraine and muscle-contraction headache entities is of dubious value."[4]

What causes muscle-contraction headache?

Anything that can cause painful, sustained contraction of neck and scalp muscles and fibrous tissue can cause headache. These abnormalities can be due to many causes. Most people who have headaches are aware that on at least some occasions, headache can be precipitated or aggravated by emotional reactions such as anxiety, anger, frustration, fear, and worry. This may also be true of migraine. Astute observers at least as far back as in the time of Plato have been aware of this.[5] Ziegler states, however, "It cannot be assumed that headache resulting from emotional stress is consistently produced by muscle contraction nor conversely that head and neck discomfort from muscle contraction is always produced by emotional tension."[6] Ziegler found that stress correlates poorly with the tension headache pattern.

Not all headaches resulting from abnormal contraction of neck muscles and fibrous tissue are caused by emotional disturbances. There are many other causes. One of these is working or performing any other activity in a position with the head constantly bent forward or turned to the side, as is often the case of bookkeepers, stenographers, architects, assembly line workers, and persons in many other occupations such as working at a computer terminal. In order to maintain the head and neck in a forward flexed position, the neck muscles are in a continuous state of contraction. If this muscle activity is sustained long enough, the neck muscles become fatigued and painful. This is a common cause of headache. Headache and muscle spasm may often be prevented by simply stretching the muscles periodically and assuming a more comfortable position.

There is a whole group of abnormalities of the neck that commonly produce neck muscle spasm and which can cause headache. These include arthritis of the neck; herniated intervertebral discs in the cervical area; head and neck injuries; and in occasional cases, infections and tumors of the neck. Pain associated with these conditions often results in protective muscle spasm caused by an attempt to limit movement of the head and neck and thus decrease neck pain. Frequently these tight neck muscles themselves become a source of pain and headache. Herniated intervertebral discs at any level in the neck and also degenerative arthritis of the vertebrae can cause headache. Surgical correction of these conditions often relieves this problem.[7, 8, 9]

MUSCLE SPASM IN THE NECK AND SCALP

These headaches can be located in any part of the head and are often difficult to distinguish from muscle-contraction headaches that can be due to emotional disturbances. In any case, if prolonged muscle contraction occurs the fibrous tissue that holds the muscles in place will shorten. When this happens it may take weeks or even months to restore normal mobility and get rid of headache.

Several years ago a medical research investigator named Cyriax found that injection of concentrated salt solution into the neck muscles in the area where the head and neck join produced headache which radiated around the head and was of maximum severity in the temple and the frontal area over the eye.[10] Injection of salt solution an inch below this area caused pain in the back of the head which extended to the top of the head; but when injected still lower in the neck, this irritant solution produced neck pain only. A neurosurgeon named Cloward injected concentrated salt solution into the intervertebral discs of the neck and found that pain occurred in the neck, shoulder, arm, but never in the head.[11] So even the headache associated with herniated discs appears to be due to neck muscle and fibrous tissue shortening rather than abnormality of the disc itself. Headaches caused by experimentally injecting salt solution into the base of the skull near its attachment to the neck, and also those due to herniated discs in the neck, and even headaches of typical muscle-contraction type related to emotional tension can be temporarily relieved by injecting a local anesthetic into the tender, contracted neck muscles. The common denominator of headaches related to disease of the neck, as well as those due to emotional disturbances, appears to be neck muscle spasm and contraction of fibrous tissue. Headache due to any of these causes can be very severe and very persistent. If persons with muscle-contraction headache are properly examined for the presence of limitation of head and neck movement, as described in chapter 2, the cause of the headache is often easily identified. There is a strong correlation between headache and persistent contraction of neck muscles and fibrous tissue regardless of whether or not emotional stress, head injury, or other factors are causing the neck muscle and fibrous tissue shortening.

Unfortunately it is believed by many otherwise knowledgeable physicians that anyone who has headaches related to muscle spasm is an emotionally disturbed person. It is often believed that the muscle contraction is secondary to the headache rather than its cause, and further, that these headaches in many cases are not completely genuine; therefore, they are scarcely worthy of medical attention. Patients who have them are often made to feel guilty for even having this kind of headache. On the other hand, common migraine headaches are considered to be a respectable type of headache since they are due to instability of the blood vessels. This unfortunate view still persists in spite of the fact that it has been demonstrated that there is no clear difference between common migraine and muscle-contraction headache. Furthermore, these headaches may be produced by the same mechanisms and they can be of equal severity. Headaches diagnosed as common migraine and muscle-contraction headache together account for the majority of common headaches. In most cases they can be successfully treated by getting rid of the abnormally contracted structures of the neck.

MUSCLE SPASM IN THE NECK AND SCALP

The mechanism by which abnormalities in the neck and the junction area between the head and neck can cause headache has been discussed by Edmeads.[12] He states that the concept that this can occur is an old one. He refers to John Helton who wrote about this relationship more than a hundred years ago. This view has been supported by many physicians since then but it has never gained such wide acceptance as has the unproven theory that abnormalities of blood vessels are the cause of most headaches. One of the reasons for this has been lack of a test that can identify those persons in whom neck abnormalities cause headaches and also lack of effective treatment for this condition. Such a test is now available and the treatment described in chapter 2 is effective for most of those who have this kind of headache. This new test identifies abnormalities that are not found during the usual physical examination or by any laboratory or x-ray study. Nor can this information be obtained by computed tomography or magnetic resonance imaging. This test is easy to perform but to be useful it must be done exactly as described in chapter 2.

Edmeads[12] gives the following criteria that are necessary to demonstrate that neck disorders cause headache: (1) there should be pain-sensitive structures within the neck; (2) there should be an identifiable abnormality of neck function that can stimulate pain receptors in this region; and (3) there should be identifiable neurologic pathways and mechanisms by which pain originating in the neck can be referred to the head. The first two criteria are well known. Nearly all the structures in the neck are pain sensitive. Further, many abnormalities that occur in the neck including arthritis, disc disease, infections, tumors, neck injuries, and muscle spasm from whatever cause including muscle tension from emotional stress can produce headache.

The work of Cyriax[10] shows that painful abnormalities in neck muscles and fibrous tissue cause headache but does not demonstrate how this occurs. The pathways by which pain is referred from the neck to the head are not well known, but it is true that compression, irritation, inflammation, or damage of any other kind to the second cervical nerve root or its sensory branch can cause pain in the back of the head. Headache in this area can often be relieved by blocking the greater occipital nerve with a local anesthetic. This nerve, which is a branch of the second cervical nerve root, supplies sensation to the back of the head.

It is more difficult to understand the mechanism by which pain is referred from the upper portion of the neck to the forehead or around the eye even though this is known to occur. It is not widely known but there is a branch of the first cervical sensory nerve root which when stimulated produces pain in the region of the eye, the forehead, and the top of the head. This has been demonstrated by Kerr.[13] The course of the sensory branch of the first cervical nerve which some have considered non-existent has been described by Kubik and Manestar.[14]

It is now recognized that abnormalities in the neck and the junction area between the head and neck can cause headache in any part of the head. Furthermore, there is a high correlation between the presence of and the severity of headache with degree of abnormal contraction of neck muscle and fibrous tissue regardless of what causes them. Treatment designed to correct these abnormalities in the neck gets rid of headache in 90 percent of cases in which

MUSCLE SPASM IN THE NECK AND SCALP

headache is not due to serious disease such as tumor, hemorrhage, infection, or serious emotional disturbances.[15]

This welcome and useful information provides a method by which most persons with common headache can get relief from this condition by getting rid of its cause rather than by chronic use of drugs. The headaches that are most responsive to this therapy are those following head and neck injuries, those caused by arthritis or chronic degenerated intervertebral discs in the neck, and those related to persistent muscle contraction and fibrous tissue shortening, whatever their cause. It is also effective in overcoming most headaches that have been diagnosed as common migraine.

These headaches should be called myofascial headaches rather than muscle-contraction headache because it is not only the muscles that are stiff and painful but also the fascia (this is the fibrous tissue that holds the muscles together) is stiff and shortened. This reduces mobility of the neck. Stiff contracted muscles can be stretched in a few days but fibrous tissue is difficult to stretch, so for this reason it may take several weeks or months to regain normal range of movement. The only satisfactory way to accomplish this is by the method of neck mobilization described in chapter 2.

Different view of muscle-contraction headache.

Not everyone shares these views. Diamond, a headache authority who had a large headache clinic in Chicago, has written that muscle-contraction headache or tension headache could better or more correctly be called "psychogenic headache."[16] He divides muscle-contraction headache, or psychogenic headache, into three separate categories. The first type of psychogenic headache is conversion headache, which he considers to be mild, moderate, or severe; either generalized or unilateral; and oftentimes associated with pain in the neck, shoulders, and arms. He believes that those who have this condition have personality traits which lead them to overreact and desire attention. Furthermore, since there is secondary gain from the headache, they might be worse off if their headaches were cured. In other words, they achieve some advantage (either emotional or material) by having their headache. His second category is that of delusional headache. These headaches are common in adolescents, but they even can be present in early childhood. They are more common in women than in men. The description of the pain is often bizarre, and the pain may be accompanied by hallucinations. He finds that these patients need psychiatric treatment. His third category is that of depressive headache. This category of headache includes the majority of individuals with "psychogenic" headache. He leaves little latitude for emotionally stable persons to have muscle-contraction headache; and his categories of muscle-contraction, or "psychogenic" headache are the same as those found in mental illness. It is a tragedy that doctors who treat headache hold this view.

According to Kudrow, "Tension headache in its varied forms is probably the most common headache and few people are spared from having this problem."[17] If this is true and if one accepts Diamond's view of tension or muscle-contraction headache, one would have to conclude that mental illness and severe emotional disturbances are extremely common and that a very large proportion of the population

MUSCLE SPASM IN THE NECK AND SCALP

is so affected. This seems to be a rather severe and unjust indictment of the majority of people who have headache.

Ryan and Ryan — ear, nose, and throat specialists who wrote a book about headache — present another view.[18] They classify muscle-contraction headache as a type of vascular headache. They suspect that the cause of the headache is reduced blood supply brought on by reflex constriction of blood vessels rather than by dilation of blood vessels, which is thought by some to be the cause of migraine. But they also state, "Headache of conversion reaction is thought to be clinically indistinguishable from muscle-contraction headache. The conversion reaction usually meets the immediate needs of the patient and is associated with obvious secondary gain." Thus they apparently believe that persons with muscle-contraction headache want to have headaches rather than wanting to get relief from them. It is no small wonder that headaches are so poorly treated by some physicians if they hold unwarranted views like this.

It can be readily seen that there is a great deal of difference of opinion, even among "authorities" on the subject of headache, as to whether muscle-contraction headache is due to physical causes or emotional factors. Consider the dilemma of the poor headache sufferer when he seeks medical attention. Even when he goes to some of the famous headache centers in the land he may be given a respectable diagnosis of common migraine by one physician; but with identical symptoms and clinical presentation in another clinic or doctor's office he may be given a diagnosis of psychogenic headache. In this case he may be considered to be having pain that is entirely imaginary or to be using his headache for secondary gain.

RELIEF FROM HEADACHE

The fact that emotional problems and everyday stresses cause headache, and that these headaches can be worsened by emotional factors, should not be construed to imply that these headaches are not real. Nor is it correct to believe that a person's headaches are entirely emotionally based if he has tight, tender neck muscles. Raskin and Appenzeller state, "Features formerly believed to be specific for tension headache such as muscle contraction and its precipitation by stress and anxiety are now known to occur just as often in migraine" as they do in tension headache.[19] Since muscle-contraction (or tension) headache is so common, and since many authorities recognize that there is no clear distinction between muscle-contraction headache and common migraine, it seems unfortunate that some "authorities" still refer to this condition as psychogenic headache and assume that those who have it are either delusional, depressed, or seeking some material or emotional gain by either pretending to have headaches or imagining that they have headaches.

Treatment.

Patients with muscle-contraction headaches have been poorly treated by most physicians. This is because there has been too much dependence on drug treatment for symptomatic relief rather than on the principle of getting rid of the cause of headache.

The simplest drug treatment for muscle-contraction headache consists of the use of over-the-counter, pain-killing medication. If these drugs do not give relief, some physicians prescribe more potent pain killers (such as codeine,

MUSCLE SPASM IN THE NECK AND SCALP

Darvon, and even Talwin). These drugs can be helpful acutely; but they should be used with caution since they can cause drug dependence, in which case the patient may be worse off because of the treatment than he was before he used these medications.

Muscle relaxants and tranquilizers are commonly used. These include Librium, Valium, meprobamate, Serax, Xanax, Ativan, and many others. These drugs also have a small but definite risk of dependency; and if they are used frequently, tolerance develops so that their dosage has to be increased to produce an effect. This is not desirable in conditions such as muscle-contraction headache or common migraine which can last for months or years if treatment consists of the use of medication only. These drugs should not be used on a daily basis for chronic headache.

Another common kind of treatment is the use of antidepressants. These drugs, of which Elavil is a commonly used example, can provide some relief from headache by a drug action that seems to be in addition to and separate from their antidepressant effect. Although many types of drugs may provide some benefit in treatment of muscle-contraction headaches, no medication program is completely satisfactory for the majority of people with this problem. Drugs do not get rid of the muscle spasm and fibrous tissue contraction that are causing the headache. Even the ergot drugs, which some physicians consider to be beneficial for migraine only, have been found helpful in treatment of muscle-contraction (or tension) headache.[20, 21] Even though these medications do provide symptomatic relief, it is far better to remove the cause for the headache rather than depend on chronic drug use.

RELIEF FROM HEADACHE

There are some traditional physical methods of treating migraine and muscle-contraction headache, but they are not very successful. Biofeedback is often used and it has been reported by some physicians to be effective. When controlled studies of the results of biofeedback on muscle-contraction headaches have been done, however, the results have been disappointing. It does not appear to be a very good treatment for large numbers of patients with any kind of headache. Not only because it is not very effective, but because it is time-consuming and costly. Raskin and Appenzeller state, "In our experience benefits (of biofeedback) have been short-lived and overall disappointing."[19] They further state, "Relaxation training appears to be more promising in that patients can continue to practice at home with occasional reinforcement from the physician without instrumentation." But they believe that: "The mainstay of therapy for tension headache, however, is pharmacotherapy. . . ."

Several physicians, including Warner and Lance, have obtained good results in treating muscle-contraction headache with relaxation methods.[22] Although there are many different programs for relaxation therapy — some taught individually, some in group sessions, and some by utilizing tape recordings for playback — the general principle of all of them is to teach mental and physical relaxation. Other commonly used physical measures include heat application, massage, diathermy, chiropractic manipulation, and acupuncture. These kinds of treatment have been reported to be beneficial in some cases, but none of them have proven to be very effective for the majority of people with muscle-contraction headache or common migraine.

MUSCLE SPASM IN THE NECK AND SCALP

Kudrow states, "Neck exercise or physical therapy other than the application of heat packs or light massage will afford little benefit and may in fact aggravate the headache by further stimulating the contracted muscles."[17] This may actually be true of some exercise programs. It may happen in some cases in which the maneuver sometimes referred to as the "yoga" head and neck rotation exercise is used. Headache and pain may be increased if there are arthritic changes or degenerated discs in the neck. This may also occur in the case of those who have had neck injuries. Overhead traction may be of some help to a few individuals, but its chief drawback is that it does not stretch the muscles and fibrous tissue in the right place. Stretching the muscles on the side of the neck by pulling the head and neck toward the shoulder, as advocated in some neck stretching exercise programs, does not effectively stretch the muscles and fibrous tissue that are causing the headache. In some cases this may actually aggravate the neck pain and headache. That is rarely true of the neck mobilization program described in chapter 2. If pain is initially increased this is usually of short duration.

Traditional medicine has overemphasized vascular causes of headache; and there has been an unfortunate neglect in recognizing the importance of painful, contracted muscles and fibrous tissue of the neck as the most common cause of chronic headache. Given this preoccupation on the part of many physicians with the idea that nearly all legitimate headaches are caused by blood vessel abnormalities, it is understandable that most persons with chronic headaches are not effectively treated by headache clinics

RELIEF FROM HEADACHE

and medical practitioners. When these patients respond poorly to treatment, they are told they will have to learn to live with their headaches. Headache sufferers are then left to shift for themselves — becoming dependent on over-the-counter pain killers or treatment by chiropractors, acupuncturists, hypnotists, and other types of practitioners.

There will always be a need for ergot preparations, Inderal, Sansert, Elavil, pain-killing medication, tranquilizers, and other kinds of medication in the acute treatment of common migraine and muscle-contraction headache as well as many other kinds of headache. These substances are helpful until the cause of headache can be eliminated. But these medications do not adequately relieve most people with persistent or frequently recurring headache because they do not remove its cause. The greatest need of the millions of people who suffer from common headache is knowledge of how they can get rid of the cause of this problem rather than depending on symptomatic treatment with continued use of pain killing drugs and tranquilizers. A simple effective means of accomplishing this objective without the danger of serious side effects of drugs or of drug dependence is explained in chapter 2.

MUSCLE SPASM IN THE NECK AND SCALP

References for Chapter 3.

1. Pozniak-Patewicz E. "Cephalgic" spasm of head and neck muscles. Headache 1976; 14:261-266.
2. Bakal DA, Kaganov JA. Muscle contraction and migraine headache: Psychophysiologic comparison. Headache 1977;17:208-215.
3, Raskin NH, Appenzeller O. Headache. Vol XIX in the series: Major problems in internal medicine. Philadelphia: WB Saunders Co, 1980:183.
4. Zeigler DK. Chronic recurring headache. American Academy of Neurology Annual Course No. 107, Modern Management of Headache 1982:34.
5. Kunkle EC. Mechanisms of headache. In: Friedman AP, Merritt HH. Headache diagnosis and treatment. Philadelphia: FA Davis Co. 1963:3.
6. Ziegler DK. Chronic recurrent headache. American Academy of Neurology Annual Course No. 107, Modern Management of Headache 1982:33-35.
7. Peterson DI, Austin GM, Dayes LA. Headache associated with discogenic disease of the cervical spine. Bull Los Angeles Neurol Soc 1975;40:96-100.
8. Raney AA, Raney RB. Headache: a common symptom of cervical disk lesions, report of cases. Arch Neurol Psychiat 1948;59:603-621.
9. Sheldon KW. Headache patterns and cervical nerve root compression – a 15-year study of hospitalization for headache. Headache 1967;6:180-188.
10. Cyriax J. Rheumatic headache. Brit Med J. 1938;2:1367.
11. Cloward RB. Cervical discography: a contribution to the etiology and mechanism of neck, shoulder and arm pain. Ann Surg 1959;150:1052-1064.
12. Edmeads J. The cervical spine and headache. Neurology 1988;38:1874-1878.
13. Kerr FWL. A mechanism to account for frontal headache in cases of posterior fossa tumors. J. Neurosurg 1961;18:605-609.
14. Kubik S, Manestar M. The role of the suboccipital nerve in the sensory inervation of the occipital region. 10th Int. Cong. Anat. Tokyo 1975;224.
15. Peterson DI. Headache — Modern concepts of diagnosis and management. Prim Care 1984; 11:707-721.
16. Diamond S. Psychogenic headache: treatment, including biofeedback techniques. In: Appenzeller O, ed. Pathogenesis and treatment of headache. New York: Spectrum Publications, Inc, 1976:131-141.
17. Kudrow L. Tension headache (scalp muscle contraction headache). In: Appenzeller O, ed. Pathogeneis and treatment of headache. New York: Spectrum Publications, Inc, 1976:81-91.
18. Ryan RE, Sr, Ryan RE, Jr. Headache and head pain — diagnosis and treatment. St.Louis: The CV Mosby Co, 1978:176-207.
19. Raskin NH, Appenzeller O. Headache. Vol XIX in the series: Major problems in

internal medicine. Philadelphia: WB Saunders Co, 1980:172-184.
20. Barrie MA, Fox WR, Weatherall M, et al. Analysis of symptoms of patients with headaches and their response to treatment with ergot derivatives. Quart J Med 1968;37:319-336.
21. Horton BT, Ryan R, Reynolds JL. Clinical observations on the use of E.C. 110, a new agent for the treatment of headache. Mayo Clin Proc 1948; 23:105-108.
22. Warner G. Lance JW. Relaxation therapy in migraine and chronic tension headache. Med J. Aust 1975;1:298-301.

4

Chronic Headache Following Head and Neck Injury

Post-trauma headache.

Headache is a common symptom following head injury. Initially, there is pain at the site of the injury — but in addition, generalized headache is often present. Many individuals who have head trauma get over their headaches within two or three weeks as the acute effects of the injury subside, but in many others this is not the case. It is estimated that one-third to one-half of persons who sustain a head injury have persistent headache for months or even years. This is true of many individuals who have impairment of function due to severe head wounds, but it is equally true in the case of many individuals who have relatively minor head trauma and no associated impairment of function. In some cases the headache becomes such a problem that it is disabling even when there is no objective evidence of abnormality resulting from the injury. It is a common medical observation that the severity of the post-trauma headache correlates poorly with the severity of the head injury. It is not uncommon for those who sustain seemingly insignificant head trauma to be incapacitated because of headache. On the other hand, those who have serious head trauma that causes loss of consciousness for several days or several weeks, and even those who have large hemorrhages in their heads that have to be treated surgically, may have little or no residual headache.

It is estimated that there are about 1.5 million serious head injuries each year in the United States, and there is a much larger number of minor head injuries. It can be readily seen that post-trauma headache is a serious problem that frequently occurs in our mechanized society. This is true for several reasons. The pain and discomfort of the headache as well as the loss of productivity are a problem to the individual who has the headache, but the disruption of family life and the financial burden to society are also major problems.

It should be stated that there are many complications of head injuries that are much more serious than headache. These complications include convulsions, paralysis, loss of ability to speak, loss of vision, impairment of mental function, and even persistent coma. These subjects will not be included in this discussion of post-trauma headache.

Post-trauma headache is similar to muscle-contraction headache.

Headache following head trauma has no specific characteristics to differentiate it from other kinds of headache. In many cases, post-trauma headache assumes characteristics that are like a combination of migraine and muscle-contraction headache. In a few cases, what would otherwise appear to be classic migraine preceded by a visual warning and characterized by unilateral throbbing headache first begins after head injury; but in a majority of cases the headache is diffuse and persistent. It may be throbbing or nonthrobbing, and it can be located in any part of the head. Usually its characteristics are more like those of muscle-contraction headache or myofascial headache than they are like classic migraine.

Postconcussion syndrome.

Frequently other symptoms are associated with post-trauma headache. These characteristically consist of dizziness, fatigue, increased perspiration, weakness, abdominal distress (including nausea and vomiting), and a whole host of other symptoms, some of which suggest emotional instability. These include nervousness, irritability, outbursts of anger, fear, anxiety, lack of confidence, inability to perform normal activities, emotional lability, and (especially in the male) decrease or loss of sexual function. After injury when several of these symptoms appear along with the headache, the entire syndrome is referred to as postconcussion syndrome if loss of consciousness occurred at the time of the injury. In some cases, similar symptoms occur after minor head injury or injury to other parts of the body even if there is no known damage to the head or neck. This may be called post-trauma syndrome. These symptoms can occur in children as well as in adults. It is not uncommon for a child who falls and bumps his head on the ice while skating or who sustains an injury in some athletic event or in an automobile accident to be incapable of continuing school and performing normal activities for several months to a year, even though no evidence of serious injury is found.

The cause of headache in postconcussion syndrome is poorly understood. In some cases of head injury there is serious brain damage, but as mentioned above, symptoms of post-concussion syndrome seem to be just as frequent, if not more frequent, in individuals who have no evidence of intracranial damage as in those who do. Many research studies have been done in an effort to try to determine why postconcussion syndrome and headache occur.

Some investigators have found abnormalities in the electroencephalogram. Others have found changes in blood flow; and still others have demonstrated abnormalities by various other tests, but these abnormalities are not consistently present after head injury. In general, these tests have not provided great insight into the problem of post-trauma headache or postconcussion syndrome.

Since most individuals who have post-trauma headache have headache characteristics similar to those of common migraine and muscle-contraction headache, it is likely that the great majority of post-trauma headaches arise from structures outside the skull rather than from abnormalities of the brain.

In many cases of head injury, there are associated injuries of the neck. In some cases these injuries are severe and consist of fractures and dislocations. In most cases, however, they are not serious and consist chiefly of soft-tissue damage, causing muscle spasm, pain, and limitation of movement of the head and neck. These abnormalities are the cause of the headaches that follow head injury in most cases. In many cases of so called "whiplash injury" there is neck stiffness and loss of normal range of motion.

Insurance and disability may increase symptoms.

Since many head and neck injuries result from motor vehicle accidents and on-the-job injuries, economic factors related to insurance compensation, disability benefits, and damages that are often sought by legal action are factors in prolonging symptoms in some cases. It can be said with complete confidence that these factors cause significant exaggeration of symptoms for secondary gain in some individuals. So-called "whiplash injuries" are very common. Usually there is no x-ray evidence of damage or external evidence of injury. It is a common observation that these injuries nearly always occur in those who are not at fault in the accident, while the driver of the car who is at fault rarely has these problems. This undoubtedly is due in part to the different mechanisms of the injury in that the vehicle not at fault in the accident is often struck from the rear. The occupants of that vehicle have hyperextension-type injuries, whereas the individuals in the car behind usually have flexion-type injuries.

No one who has had experience with industrial accident cases and traffic injuries would deny that there are large numbers of individuals who exaggerate their symptoms in the hope of receiving monetary gain. In these cases, symptoms often improve when insurance settlement is made. However, it is equally certain that this is not true of many persons who have post-trauma headache. Many of these individuals have sustained injuries in the home and in other situations in which they are not covered by insurance and have no hope of getting any compensation. Some of these persons have long periods of inability to perform normal activity because of post-trauma headache. In some cases it is difficult to determine which symptoms after injury are genuine and which are due to exaggeration of the effects of injury.

Treatment of post-trauma headache.

No completely satisfactory method of treating persons with post-trauma headache and postconcussion syndrome has been found. Initially it is important to rule out the presence of serious effects of injuries such as brain or spinal cord damage, fractures, or hemorrhages. After this has been done, many of the measures that have been found beneficial in treatment of muscle-contraction or myofascial headache are very successful in treating headache following head and neck injuries. Simple analgesics — such as aspirin, Anacin, Tylenol, Excedrin, and other similar preparations — can be used. Most potent prescription drugs — such as codeine, Darvon, and Fiorinal — are often needed. Antidepressants, such as Elavil, may also be helpful.

If pain and muscle spasm of the neck muscles are present, the use of a soft neck collar for support of the head and neck can be beneficial. This kind of support is usually most helpful when the patient is performing some activity that requires forward bending of the head and neck in activities such as ironing, vacuuming, or any kind of desk work. The purpose of the collar is to support the weight of the head so that the painful neck muscles can relax.

CHRONIC HEADACHE FOLLOWING HEAD INJURY

Use of a neck collar to stabilize the head and neck while a person is sleeping is also helpful in decreasing pain and headache in persons who awaken during the night because of these symptoms. This is also true for those who awaken each morning with headache. The collar should not be so thick that it hyperextends the neck. It should not be worn continuously unless some specific injury, such as fracture or dislocation, is present. Heat, massage, and other forms of physical therapy are beneficial. Some physicians have found that medications commonly used in the treatment of chronic headache — including Elavil, inderal, and even some of the ergot preparations — are useful in treatment of post-trauma headache.

In several respects, post-trauma headaches are similar to muscle-contraction headache. Neck pain and muscle spasm are frequently present, and neck mobility is limited. If the limited neck movement is chiefly that of decrease of rotation and lateral bending, good relief from post-trauma headache can usually be obtained from the neck-stretching exercises for treatment of muscle-contraction headache described in chapter 2. The muscle stretching exercise should be done gently and only after fracture and dislocation have been ruled out. It must be done exactly as described to obtain maximum benefit.

Accidents and injuries may cause serious emotional disturbances. This may be especially true if other individuals in the accident have been seriously injured or killed. Even if there have been no serious injuries, emotional problems — including fear, anxiety, and other stresses related to the associated social and financial problems — may be present. In some cases psychiatric treatment

RELIEF FROM HEADACHE

may be necessary. In other cases reassurance that no serious abnormality is present and treatment of headache and other symptoms by methods mentioned above, along with encouragement to return to a normal lifestyle as soon as possible, are helpful.

The most successful method of management of post-trauma headache is gradual neck mobilization to restore normal range of motion as describe in chapter 2.

5

Brain Tumors Can Cause Headache

There are several kinds of brain tumors.

Brain tumors, including those which arise from inside the head and those that spread to the brain from other parts of the body, usually cause headache. About half of all brain tumors are secondary or metastatic tumors that arise in other parts of the body and spread to the brain through the blood stream. Thirty to 50 percent of these metastatic brain tumors arise from the lung; but malignant tumors from other locations — including breast, colon, and kidney — also frequently spread to the brain. This may happen even before the primary tumor is suspected. Tumors of the uterus and tumors of the skin, other than malignant melanoma, hardly ever metastasize to the brain. But malignant melanoma arising in the skin spreads to the brain in 80 to 90 percent of cases.

Tumors that arise inside the head can be either malignant or nonmalignant (benign). Both malignant and nonmalignant tumors can produce similar types of symptoms, but the malignant tumors usually progress much more rapidly than those that are nonmalignant. Symptoms from tumors located inside the head can be produced in several different ways. They may be due to direct pressure on pain-sensitive structures, destruction of pain-sensitive structures, or by stretching of pain-sensitive tissue. It is by the latter means that most intracranial tumors produce headache (Figure 1). Headaches due to brain tumor are usually slowly progressive over a period of days, weeks, or months; and in the case of some benign tumors symptoms may progress over a period of several years before the tumor is diagnosed. Even though some brain tumors grow slowly, some of their symptoms, including headache, may come on very rapidly. This can happen if there is hemorrhage into the tumor or if the tumor causes sudden obstruction of the outflow of cerebrospinal fluid from the ventricles of the brain where most of this fluid is produced.

Brain tumor headache may in some cases be similar to headaches of other kinds such as migraine and tension headache. For this reason, special x-ray testing may be necessary to determine the cause of this symptom. Headache from brain tumor is usually of a changing pattern in that it may become progressively more severe and more frequent. In a few cases the headache is continuous, but more frequently it is intermittent. Although some brain tumors cause excruciating headache, this is not always true; and some persons who have brain tumors have no headache throughout the entire course of their disease. It can be stated with confidence, however, that at least 80 to 90 percent of patients with brain tumor have headaches at some time during their illness. And at least 10 percent of persons with brain tumor experience headache as one of their initial symptoms. Frequently persons with brain tumors have nearly continuous mild

BRAIN TUMORS CAN CAUSE HEADACHE

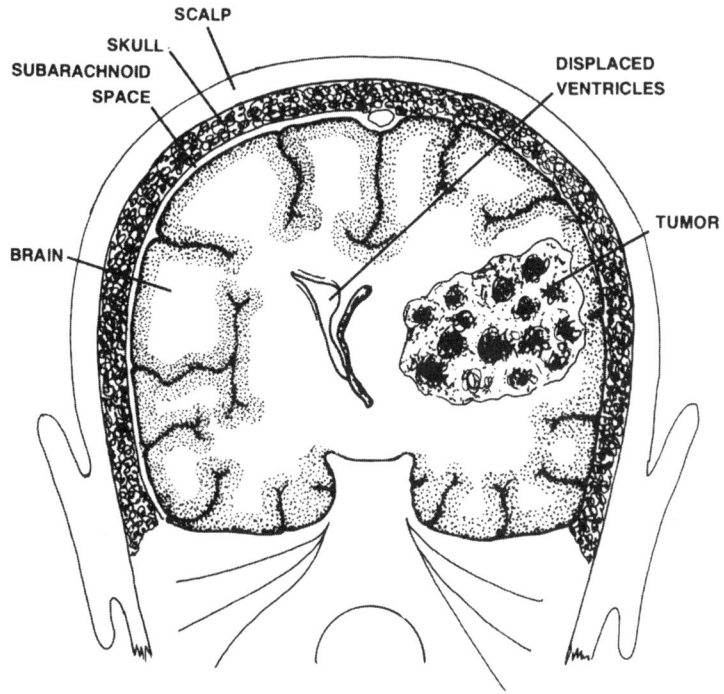

Figure 1. Sketch illustrating the mechanism by which brain tumors produce some of their symptoms. Headache results from stretching of pain-sensitive structures due to progressive enlargement of the tumor. Other symptoms of brain tumors may result from destruction of brain tissue. The illustration shows the relationship of the scalp, skull, and brain (containing a brain tumor) and what they would look like if a coronal section of the entire head was made by sectioning through both ears.

headache with superimposed bursts of severe headache that last from a few seconds to a few hours.

Headaches caused by brain tumors may awaken a person in the middle of the night with severe pain, but brain tumor headaches make up a very small percent of those headaches which awaken persons from sleep. More common causes of headaches that awaken a person from sleep include muscle-contraction headache, cluster headache, glaucoma, abnormalities of the cervical spine (including arthritis and neck injuries), and depression. Although headache associated with depression usually does not awaken a person from a sound sleep, it is often present when a person with this condition awakens during the night or in the early morning hours. When this happens it may be difficult to determine if the headache is the cause of awakening or if it is only present when awakening occurs.

If a brain tumor is close to the surface of the brain it may cause headache directly over the area where the tumor is located, but in most instances the location of the headache bears little relationship to the location of the tumor. For example, a tumor in the back of the brain may cause headache over one eye. Frequently headache associated with a brain tumor is not localized at all, but rather it is felt all over the head.

Brain tumor headache as well as other symptoms may be produced by stretching of large arteries at the base of the brain or some of the arteries, veins, and sinuses of the meninges that cover the brain. When a tumor causes increased pressure in the head, headache may result from enlargement and distention of the ventricles, which causes stretching of pain-sensitive structures. In this case the headache is usually generalized and may be present over the entire head, but sometimes it is most severe in the frontal areas. However, it has been demonstrated experimentally that increasing the pressure inside the head does not of itself

BRAIN TUMORS CAN CAUSE HEADACHE

cause headache. This experiment has been done by putting extra fluid into the subarachnoid space and into the ventricles to cause increase in pressure. Headache results only if there is stretching of pain sensitive structures associated with the increase in intracranial pressure. If the intracranial pressure gets too high from any cause, it results in death by interfering with blood flow to the brain and by compressing the vital centers in the brain stem.

Brain tumors cause many kinds of symptoms.

Headache can be a first symptom of brain tumor in some cases; but usually there are other symptoms such as change in personality, partial loss of vision, impairment of function or sensation on one side of the body, loss of memory, slowing of mental function, or convulsions before the headache begins. Usually these symptoms are progressive, but the progression may be very slow — especially in the case of tumors that are not malignant. In general, the more rapidly a tumor grows, the more likely it will produce headache. This is true because a rapidly growing tumor does not allow as much time for accommodation by slow stretching of pain-sensitive structures as occurs in the case of slowly growing tumors. In some cases tumors inside the head cause sustained contraction of muscles of the neck and scalp by reflex means. This sustained contraction of muscles is an additional cause of headache. When this occurs it may suggest that the headache is due to something other than a tumor, such as arthritis of the neck, emotional stress, or one of the other causes of muscle-contraction headache.

RELIEF FROM HEADACHE

Headache caused by brain tumor may fluctuate in severity due to several different causes. The headache may be more severe when the patient is lying down than when he is standing. It is often aggravated by straining, coughing, or sneezing; but changes in severity of brain tumor headache may occur throughout the day, even if the person is at bed rest. These changes in headache severity may relate to fluctuations of pressure inside the head. Headache caused by brain tumors are not the only kinds of headache that are affected by straining, coughing, or changes in position; so change in headache due to these activities is not diagnostic of brain tumor.

Although the characteristics of headache may in some cases be suggestive of brain tumor, there is nothing about brain tumor headaches that clearly differentiates them from other kinds of headache. Of greater importance in suggesting the presence of a brain tumor than any characteristic of the headache is the presence of associated symptoms. These include impairment of mental function, poor coordination, and other abnormalities of brain function mentioned above which may be present if the headache is due to a tumor.

Special kinds of x-rays and other tests help in diagnosis.

When a brain tumor is suspected, more information to assist in diagnosis can be obtained by several tests including electroencephalography and angiography. But the most helpful tests are x-ray computed tomography (CT or CAT scanning) and magnetic resonance imaging (MRI). This is true because of the high degree of reliability and safety of these tests. Very

BRAIN TUMORS CAN CAUSE TUMORS

sophisticated imaging and computer techniques are used in performing these examinations. Pictures are obtained which look like one might imagine they would look if the entire head — including the skull, scalp, brain, and all other structures inside the head — were sliced with a large bread slicer. By means of CT and MRI scanning, tumors as well as hemorrhages and several other kinds of abnormalities inside the head can often be quickly identified with a high degree of accuracy (Figure 2).

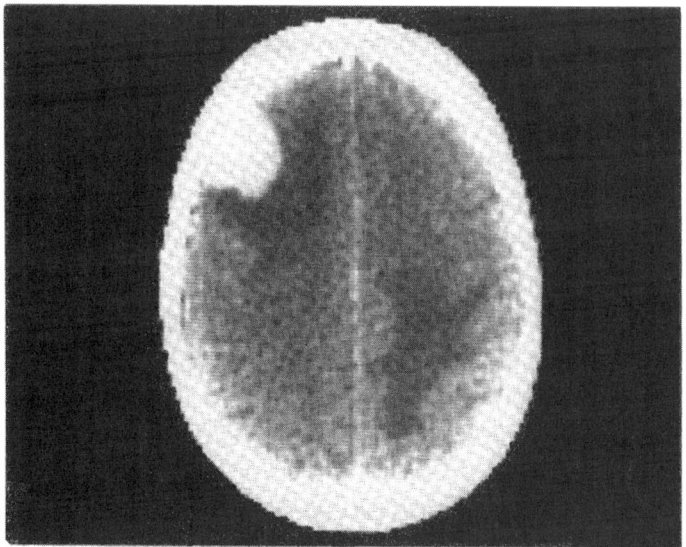

Figure 2. Computed tomogram (CT scan) of a brain tumor showing prominent distortion and stretching of intracranial structures. The large, irregular, white area is the tumor. Another smaller tumor was seen in a higher section. The dark area on the right side in the lower part of this section is edema due to the other tumor.

RELIEF FROM HEADACHE

Treatment.

After the tumor has been identified by CT or MRI scanning and supplemental information obtained by other tests, a precise diagnosis can be made by means of biopsy, or if possible, complete removal of the tumor by a neurosurgeon. Tumors that are usually not malignant (such as meningeomas, cysts, pituitary tumors, and several types of neuromas) often can be successfully removed with complete relief of the patient's symptoms — including headache. Complete and permanent cure may be obtained. Results are usually not very good in treatment of malignant tumors, but occasionally even these tumors can be completely eradicated by a combination of surgery, radiation therapy, and chemotherapy. Even if a tumor cannot be successfully eradicated, symptoms such as headache which are due to growth of the tumor can be at least partially relieved by symptomatic treatment, which consists of combating tissue swelling around the tumor and treating the increased intracranial pressure. This can be done in some cases by introducing an artificial shunt to allow the cerebrospinal fluid to flow out of the head and by treatment with several kinds of drugs that decrease brain swelling. Even though treatment of headache due to brain tumor may be successful in some cases, it is fortunate that less than one in a thousand headaches is due to this cause.

6

Headache Due to Hemorrhage Inside the Head

Causes of headache associated with intracranial hemorrhage.

Bleeding into the brain or around the brain can be due to many different causes. In nearly every case of intracranial hemorrhage there is an associated headache which is usually very severe. This headache may be produced in several different ways. If the hemorrhage is a large one, stretching of pain-sensitive structures occurs just as it does in the case of brain tumors or any other abnormal process which occupies space and causes stretching and displacement of tissues inside the head. Hemorrhage in the head, regardless of its cause, may result in irritation and inflammation of pain-sensitive structures; and this too can cause headache. Accumulation of blood at the site of the hemorrhage and also spread of blood to more distant sites inside the head can have this effect. In some cases this irritation may result in reflex spasm of neck muscles; and this also can be a cause of headache, which is in addition to that produced by the direct effects of this hemorrhage. Several of these pain-producing mechanisms may be present in any case of intracranial hemorrhage, regardless of the cause of bleeding.

Headache due to intracranial hemorrhage caused by head injury.

The most common cause of intracranial bleeding is head injury. Although this cause of bleeding is more frequent in the young and in the middle aged, it is not uncommon in the elderly. In the elderly, very minor, seemingly insignificant head injuries may in some cases produce large hemorrhages which can be fatal. Persons who have abnormalities of blood clotting such as alcohol abusers are also likely to have intracranial bleeding from relatively minor head injuries.

Hemorrhage due to head injury as well as other causes may occur in five different compartments or regions in and around the brain, and headache may be due to bleeding in any one or all of these areas. The outer covering of the brain is called the dura mater because it is formed from hard tough tissue. It is just inside the skull and actually forms a part of the inner lining of the skull. The potential space between the skull and the dura is called the epidural space, which normally has nothing in it. In some cases of head injury, especially if there is a skull fracture across one of the arteries which supplies the dura mater with blood, hemorrhage may collect in the epidural space. For this reason these hemorrhages are referred to as epidural hemorrhages. They can be rapidly fatal. Although these hemorrhages may occur in severe head injury, they also can occur in injuries that do not

HEADACHE DUE TO HEMORRHAGE INSIDE THE HEAD

at first seem to be serious. For example, if someone slips and strikes his head on a sidewalk or on the concrete apron of a swimming pool or if he receives a blow to the head from any other cause, an epidural hemorrhage may occur and progress rapidly. In most of these cases the injury is sufficiently severe to cause the victim to be immediately rendered unconscious for at least a few seconds or minutes due to the concussion or the direct effect of trauma to the brain. The injured person may then regain consciousness in a few seconds to half an hour and seem to be recovering satisfactorily. But if one of the arteries in the dura has been torn, hemorrhage may accumulate in the epidural space, causing so much pressure in the head that the victim again loses consciousness. If he is not treated very quickly by surgical removal of the blood from the epidural space, he usually will not survive. During the period of consciousness between the time when the injured person first lost consciousness from the concussion and when he again loses consciousness from increased intracranial pressure from the hemorrhage, severe headache is usually present. In some persons with epidural hemorrhage, there is no lucid interval at all. Even if there is a lucid period, the headache is often thought to be due to the direct effects of the injury; and the seriousness of the condition may not be recognized. Epidural hemorrhages are less common than hemorrhages in the other locations or compartments of the head, but it is very important to recognize them since treatment can be successful only if it is performed quickly. If not, permanent brain damage or death will usually result.

Hemorrhage due to injury may also occur in the subdural space. This is a potential space that lies between the dura on the outside and the second covering of the brain called the arachnoid on the inside. Hemorrhages in this space are called subdural hematomas. They are usually caused by bleeding from torn veins rather than from arteries, as is the case with epidural hemorrhages (Figure 1). They usually cause headache felt on the side of the head where the hemorrhage is located. Some of these hemorrhages occur in severe head injuries and can be rapidly fatal; but they also may occur in relatively minor head injuries, and in some cases there is no history of head injury at all. Subdural hemorrhages have been known to occur, especially in the elderly, from what seems to be an insignificant bump on the head and even from a jolt received from falling and landing on the buttocks. In this instance they occur because a sudden jolt causes the brain to shift in position inside the skull, tearing delicate blood vessels. Subdural hemorrhages, if they result from minor injuries, may be slowly progressive over a period of several weeks to as long as three months. If they are not recognized and treated they can be fatal. These hemorrhages occur most frequently in the elderly, in children under the age of two or three years, and in alcoholics. In small children they are one of the relatively common conditions found in battered children, and the presence of a subdural hematoma in a child should lead to suspicion of this problem.

Progressing inward, the next space where hemorrhage occurs from head injury is the subarachnoid space which lies between the arachnoid and the pia mater. The pia is a very thin membrane that is adherent to the brain tissue. Normally the subarachnoid space is filled with cerebrospinal fluid, which is a clear, watery fluid that acts as a cushion for the brain. In nearly all severe head injuries and many minor ones, the cerebrospinal fluid becomes bloody from hemorrhage

HEADACHE DUE TO HEMORRHAGE INSIDE THE HEAD

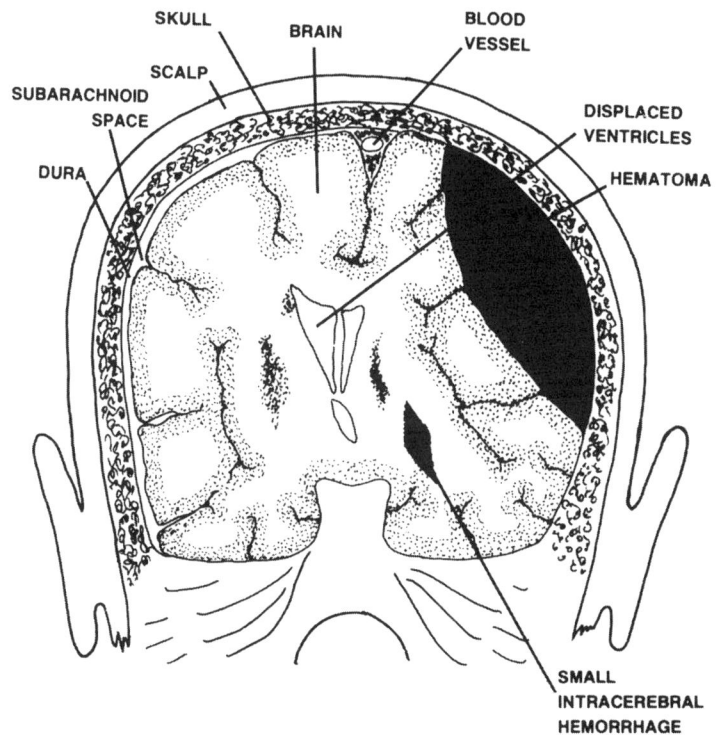

Figure 1. Subdural hematoma. Either subdural hematomas or epidural hematomas produce headache by progressive stretching of pain-sensitive tissue due to continuing hemorrhage or swelling of the blood clot.

which comes from bruised areas on the brain surface or from blood vessels which are torn as a result of the injury. A small amount of blood in the subarachnoid space may not produce headache of itself, but if a very large amount of subarachnoid hemorrhage is present it can cause headache by stretching and distention of pain-sensitive structures. Headache can also be caused by inflammation and irritation of areas that are pain-sensitive or by reflex stiffness and painful contraction of the neck muscles.

The fourth layer or compartment where hemorrhage due to injury may occur is in the brain substance itself. In most of these cases there is also bleeding into the subarachnoid space. Hemorrhage in brain tissue, if of significant degree, may produce headache by stretching and distension of blood vessels and other pain-sensitive tissues, but not by damage to the brain tissue itself since brain tissue is insensitive to pain. If a hemorrhage in brain tissue or any other area inside the head is very large, it may cause death from increased intracranial pressure which prevents adequate circulation of blood to the brain and eventually stops respiration by pressure on the brain stem.

The fifth compartment in which hemorrhage from injury occurs is within the ventricles. These normally contain clear cerebrospinal fluid. Hemorrhage into the ventricular system is nearly always secondary to bleeding which extends into the ventricles from damaged brain tissue. Hemorrhage into the ventricles is also another cause of subarachnoid hemorrhage since the cerebrospinal fluid flows from the ventricles out into the subarachnoid space. It is not uncommon in severe head injuries for hemorrhage to occur in all five locations. Injuries of this severity may be rapidly fatal.

Severe headache may also occur in cases of head injury in which there is no hemorrhage at all. Headache in this situation may be due to several mechanisms, including the direct effect of the injury — causing swelling of the brain which may occur even in the absence of hemorrhage. Associated injuries

HEADACHE DUE TO HEMORRHAGE INSIDE THE HEAD

which damage the muscles, ligaments, and other soft tissues of the head and neck may also be present and cause headache. Headaches due to head injury may be very persistent and severe even though no damaged tissue or hemorrhage is found. These are usually post-trauma muscle-contraction headaches and they can usually be successfully treated by the method described in chapter 2.

Headache caused by hemorrhage due to hypertension.

The second most common cause of hemorrhage inside the head is high blood pressure. When bleeding occurs from this cause, it is due to rupture of small blood vessels inside the brain. This results from slowly progressive, degenerative changes that weaken the walls of these blood vessels due to high blood pressure of long duration. Although the blood vessels from which these hemorrhages arise may be very small, the hemorrhages may be very large; and they are fatal in over 50 percent of cases. These hemorrhages are one of the causes of severe strokes. Depending on the size and location of the hemorrhage, loss of consciousness may occur very rapidly, but prior to loss of consciousness severe headache is usually present. This is due to stretching of pain-sensitive structures.

Hemorrhage into brain tissue due to bleeding from small blood vessels may also occur in several other diseases, including leukemia and some kinds of anemia (including sickle cell anemia). It can also result from the effects of some kinds of drugs including cocaine. Many of these hemorrhages cannot be treated very successfully because they often occur so rapidly that they produce permanent damage or death before treatment can be given. In some cases they are due to serious diseases for which treatment is not very effective (Figure 2). Occasional cases are benefited by surgery.

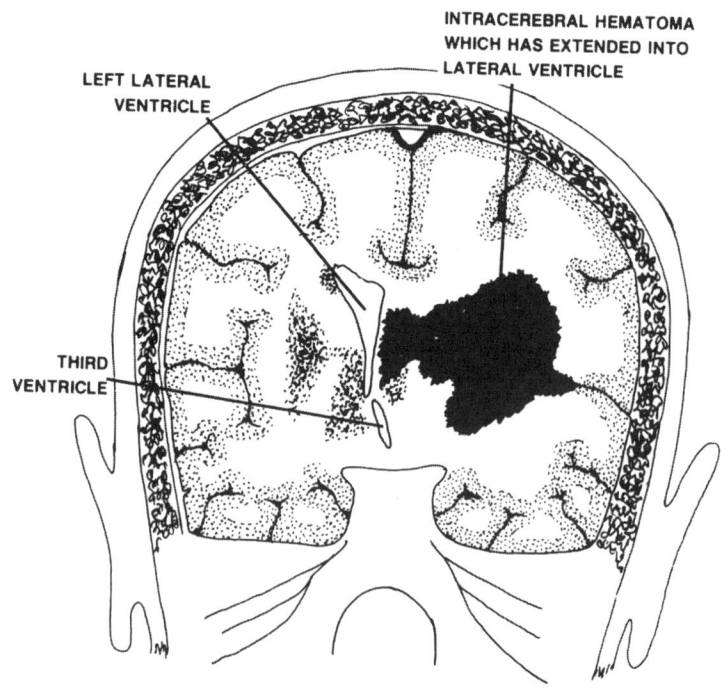

Figure 2. Intracerebral hemorrhage. Intracerebral hemorrhages usually cause sudden severe headaches before they cause loss of consciousness. These hemorrhages are usually due to the chronic effects of high blood pressure causing weakening of blood vessel walls. Most of them are fatal. In this case the intracerebral hemorrhage has extended into the ventricle.

HEADACHE DUE TO HEMORRHAGE INSIDE THE HEAD

Hemorrhages due to abnormal blood vessels.

The third most common kind of intracranial hemorrhage that may cause sudden onset of severe headache is rupture of an intracranial aneurysm. An aneurysm is an abnormal bulging of a weak area in a blood vessel which in some ways can be compared to a bulge in a defective automobile tire. These aneurysms can "blow out" just as a blowout can occur in a weakened area on a bicycle or automobile tire. They usually occur on a large blood vessel at the base of the brain so when they break open they cause bleeding into the subarachnoid space. A blowout or rupture of an intracranial aneurysm may occur at any age, even in infancy; but it is most likely to occur between the ages of forty and sixty. Even though aneurysms may not rupture until after middle age, the weakness of the blood vessel that allows the aneurysm to form and in some cases even the aneurysm itself may be present from birth. The defect in the blood vessel where an aneurysm forms is usually located where a large artery divides into two smaller ones. Intracranial aneurysms vary greatly in size, some being a little larger than a pinhead and scarcely detectable without a magnifying glass. The ones that are most likely to rupture and bleed may be as large as a bean, and the largest ones can be nearly as large as a golf ball. Large aneurysms may produce symptoms by compression and stretching of tissues inside the head even before they rupture, in the same way that a tumor can produce pressure effects and stretching of pain-sensitive tissue. The great majority of aneurysms produce no symptoms at all until they break open and bleed (Figure 3).

RELIEF FROM HEADACHE

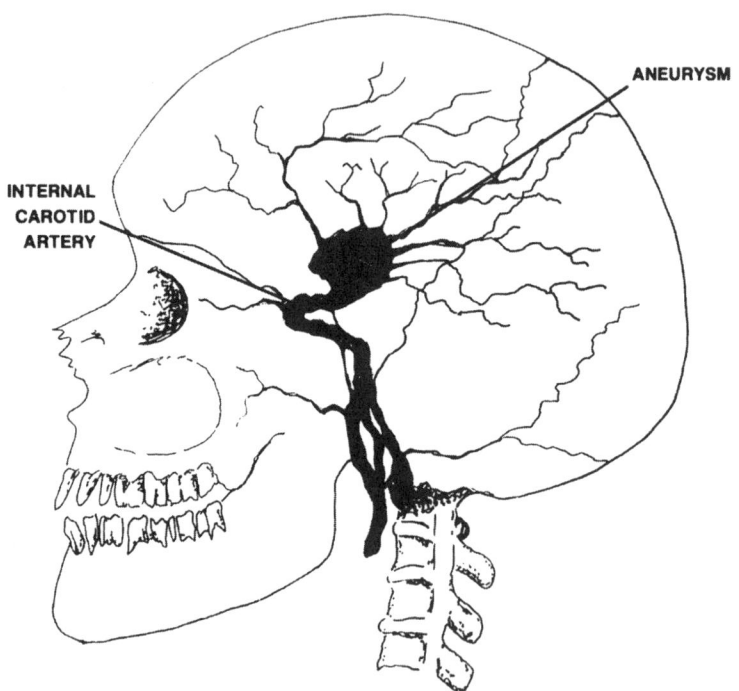

Figure 3. Giant aneurysm of the internal carotid artery. Aneurysms, regardless of size, usually do not cause headache until they rupture. When the aneurysm ruptures, severe headache results from blood spreading throughout the head. The first hemorrhage from an aneurysm is fatal in about one-third of cases. Nearly 50 percent of those who survive the first hemorrhage will die from subsequent hemorrhages in the next few months unless the aneurysm is treated surgically.

The most characteristic symptom of rupture of an aneurysm is sudden onset of severe headache which in many cases is followed by loss of consciousness. In some cases the hemorrhage occurs so rapidly and the headache comes on so sud-

HEADACHE DUE TO HEMORRHAGE INSIDE THE HEAD

denly that the patient may actually hear and feel a "bang" as the severe headache begins. For this reason some individuals with ruptured aneurysms believe after they regain consciousness that they were struck over the head by a club or some other object. They may think injury was the cause of their headache and loss of consciousness rather than a spontaneous hemorrhage in the head. Other symptoms which may occur in some cases include vomiting, impairment of vision, change in mental function, and convulsions. Depending on the location of the aneurysm, some individuals may have paralysis of one side of the body like that which occurs in a common stroke. The outcome after rupture of an aneurysm depends upon several factors. These include the size of the aneurysm before rupture, the amount of bleeding before the hemorrhage stops, and whether there are recurrent hemorrhages soon after the initial one. In one-third of cases, the first hemorrhage is fatal. In the remaining patients, symptoms slowly resolve; but there is a high incidence of recurrent hemorrhage during the next few days to several years unless the aneurysm is treated surgically to prevent this from happening.

Another kind of abnormality of blood vessels which may cause sudden hemorrhage into the subarachnoid space and which also may bleed directly into the substance of the brain itself is called a vascular malformation. There are several types of vascular malformations. These abnormalities are present from birth, but they may not produce symptoms for many years. Vascular malformations are, however, more likely than aneurysms to produce symptoms before they rupture. About one-third of them cause convulsions before they break open and cause intracranial hemorrhage. Headaches may occur from distension of the blood vessels even before rupture, but characteristically vascular malformations produce a sudden severe headache at the time they bleed. In this sense they are similar to ruptured aneurysms. The average age at which the first hemorrhage from a vascular malformation occurs is thirty-one years. Many of these persons have no warning symptoms prior to the onset of the hemorrhage. There is approximately 10 percent mortality with the first bleed; so they are less likely to cause death from the first hemorrhage than ruptured aneurysms. Vascular malformation, like aneurysms, can usually be successfully treated surgically if they can be diagnosed before severe brain damage occurs. The most characteristic symptom of ruptured intracranial vascular malformations, as is true of all types of intracranial bleeding, is sudden onset of severe headache when the hemorrhage occurs. Ruptured vascular malformations as well as ruptured aneurysms occasionally cause subdural hematomas in addition to the subarachnoid hemorrhage.

Diagnosis is made by special tests.

Diagnosis of the presence of intracranial hemorrhage and identification of the cause and site of the bleeding can usually be accomplished by special x-ray tests. Computed tomography and MRI scanning are the most effective means of diagnosing the presence of intracranial hemorrhage, but even these sophisticated tests may not detect small hemorrhages in the subarachnoid space. In these cases examination of the cerebrospinal fluid obtained by spinal puncture may be necessary for diagnosis. After the presence of hemorrhage has been established, the location and type of abnormality causing the hemorrhage can usually be determined by cerebral angiography. This is done by injecting an x-ray dense liquid so it will go into the arteries in the head to demonstrate the blood vessel abnormalities on x-ray film. X-rays are taken in rapid sequence as this x-ray dense liquid flows through the blood vessels. By this method abnormalities of blood vessels (such as aneurysms, vascular malformations, and also blood clots causing obstruction to blood flow) can be identified.

Treatment of intracranial hemorrhage is often successful if early diagnosis is accomplished, but in many cases permanent brain damage or fatality occurs before effective treatment can be given. If the intracranial hemorrhage resolves, or if it is successfully treated, the headache caused by the hemorrhage usually requires no additional treatment.

7

Headache Can Be Caused by Infections

Infections often cause headache.

Nearly any kind of infection — whether it is caused by bacteria, viruses, or other organisms — can cause headache. Severity of headaches due to infections often parallels the elevation of temperature caused by the infection. These headaches may be due to several different causes, but at least one of the principle ones is that of painful dilation of blood vessels secondary to the inflammation and the fever that accompanies the infection. Regardless of where infections are located in the body, headache frequently accompanies them. Pneumonia, viral infections like the flu, and even infection of the gastrointestinal and urinary tracts (especially if they are accompanied by high fever) often cause headache. Some kinds of systemic infections cause headache even if fever does not occur. Lyme disease in its subacute form is an example.

Infections inside the head nearly always cause severe headache.

Headache is especially likely to occur from infections

HEADACHE CAN BE CAUSED BY INFECTIONS

such as meningitis that affect the central nervous system. There are many kinds of infections of the nervous system, and frequently they are very serious and can cause death. They can be classified by their location in the same way that hemorrhages associated with head injury can be classified but they can also be categorized by the type of organism that causes the infection. Headache may be associated with infections in any part of the central nervous system.

When infection occurs between the dura and the skull, it is called an epidural abscess. Infection localized to this potential epidural space is very rare. When it occurs, it is usually secondary to extension from other locations, such as sinusitis or osteomyelitis of the skull. Infection in the subdural space is also rare, and it is usually due to the same causes that produce infection in the epidural space. Infection in the subdural space is called subdural abscess or subdural empyema. Infection which occurs in the subarachnoid space involving the cerebrospinal fluid and the surface of the brain is called meningitis. This is the most common type of infection that occurs inside the head. Headache is usually the first and one of the most characteristic symptoms of this condition.

Meningitis can be due to many difference causes, but the most common cause is viral infection. Viral meningitis in turn may be caused by many different kinds of viruses; but each of them usually produces a rather characteristic type of illness consisting of severe headache, stiffness of the neck, fever, nausea, vomiting, and generalized symptoms (such as aching and pain all over the body). Some of the more common causes of viral meningitis includes several kinds of viruses that cause "intestinal flu" and even the virus that causes mumps. In these instances the symptoms characteristic of the primary site of infection also occur and meningitis is actually a complication of these infections. Complete recovery is the rule.

Bacterial meningitis is a serious condition.

Meningitis caused by bacterial infections is usually much more serious than that caused by viruses. These infections are often fatal unless diagnosed and treated early in their course. The best-known type of bacterial meningitis is meningococcal meningitis, which is quite contagious and often occurs in epidemics. The bacteria that causes lobar pneumonia as well as several other types of bacteria may also cause meningitis. In any case of meningitis it is important to find out what kind of organism is causing the infection so that it can be treated with the most effective antibiotic medication. The diagnosis of meningitis and identification of the organism causing the infection is accomplished by examination of cerebrospinal fluid obtained by spinal puncture. Normal spinal fluid is clear and looks like water, but in cases of bacterial meningitis it may resemble pus draining from an abscess. In these cases the pus completely surrounds the brain and causes impairment of brain function and severe headache. Outcome depends to a great degree on the rapidity of diagnosis and the giving of appropriate antibiotic treatment.

Less common but just as serious is chronic meningitis. It may be due to tuberculosis or infection by a fungus, and it can be fatal in a period of a few days to a few months. Headache is usually an early symptom. If diagnosed early in its course

HEADACHE CAN BE CAUSED BY INFECTIONS

tuberculous meningitis can be treated successfully; but if not diagnosed early the usual result is severe impairment of brain function or death. The same is true of meningitis due to fungal organisms. These meningeal infections are often more difficult to treat than bacterial infection because the fungal organisms are very resistant to currently available medications. There are many other causes of meningitis, including syphilis, and even amoebae, and several other kinds of organisms. These conditions are very rare, but their symptoms, including headache, are similar to those of the more common types of meningitis. In each case successful treatment depends upon finding the cause of the infection and using the most effective medication to eliminate it.

Brain abscess.

Infections that involve brain tissue directly are of two different types. If the infection is due to bacteria, an abscess usually forms. A brain abscess is similar to an abscess in any other part of the body in that there is an accumulation of pus which causes swelling. When it is located in the brain, it causes headache and other symptoms by producing stretching and compression of pain-sensitive structures such as blood vessels and the meninges around the brain (Figure 1). Any abnormality that causes swelling inside the head can stretch pain-sensitive structures and cause headache by this means. Other symptoms can include paralysis or loss of feeling on one side of the body, impairment of speech, partial loss of vision, convulsions, and other abnormalities. A brain abscess can also cause increase in pressure inside the head

RELIEF FROM HEADACHE

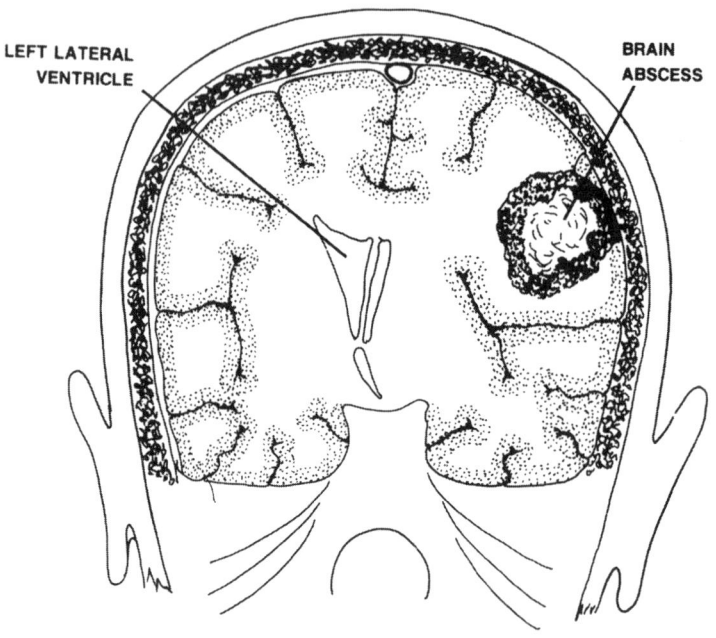

Figure 1. Brain abscess. Brain abscesses cause headache by progressive enlargement causing stretching of pain-sensitive structures. In this way they are similar to tumors or blood clots. Headaches may also be caused by irritation resulting from the infection.

in the same way that a tumor or blood clot can produce this effect, and for this reason it can be rapidly fatal.

Encephalitis.

A more common kind of central nervous system infection affecting brain tissue, but less common than meningitis,

HEADACHE CAN BE CAUSED BY INFECTIONS

is encephalitis. The term encephalitis refers to infection which affects the tissues of the brain in a diffuse manner without causing localization or abscess formation. In most cases diffuse infection of the brain is due to a virus rather than bacteria. In addition to headache, encephalitis may produce several types of abnormalities of brain function. In some cases, coma and death result due to disruption of brain cell function and swelling of brain tissue. Even though some kinds of encephalitis have a high fatality rate, other kinds of encephalitis are relatively mild and complete recovery is the rule. The most frequently occurring type of serious encephalitis is herpes simplex encephalitis which is due to the same organism that causes cold sores. Only about 5 to 10 percent of persons affected have good recovery from this disease.

Treatment of the infection usually relieves the headache.

Depending upon the type of infection and its location, headache associated with central nervous system infection may be due to any one of the mechanisms of headache production previously described. These include inflammation and irritation of pain-sensitive structures and dilation of pain-sensitive blood vessels. Both of these occur in most kinds of central nervous system infection. When abscess or brain swelling occurs the other mechanisms of pain production (such as stretching or compression of pain-sensitive tissue) also take place. Another cause of headache and pain associated with intracranial infection is reflex contraction of muscles of the neck. This produces headache due to stiffness and spasm of these tissues. Complete resolution of headache is the rule if the infection is overcome by the immune processes of the body, as is the case with many viral infections; or if the infection is satisfactorily treated with antibiotics, as in the case of bacterial infections. If an abscess is present, surgical drainage or complete removal of the abscess may be necessary.

8

Migraine: There Are Several Kinds

History.

Migraine has been recognized as a type of headache for at least two thousand years. Critchley states that Aretaeus of Cappadocia, a philosopher of Asia Minor, recognized migraine as an entity and separated it from other types of headache in the second century A.D.[1] There are historical references dating back farther than that which appear to refer to migraine, but these descriptions are less specific than that given by this philosopher. He described migraine as an intermittent headache disorder which occurred on one side of the head but which was not necessarily always on the same side and which was associated with vomiting and sensitivity to light and noise. Some believe that the word migraine is a perversion of the term "hemicrania," which was used by Galen who also lived in the second century A.D. This term is occasionally used as a synonym for migraine even today. It appears, however, that no significant progress was made in understanding this kind of headache or in treating it effectively until the twentieth century. Critchley has summarized the history of migraine during the last two thousand years.[1]

RELIEF FROM HEADACHE

The infrequency of references to migraine as well as other kinds of headache in ancient and medieval literature had led to the belief on the part of some that migraine is a condition that is relatively new in the history of mankind. Some believe that it affects chiefly the intelligent and the civilized.[2] There is no good evidence to support these views, and it appears that they are purely supposition. Rather, it is likely that prehistoric man suffered from migraine as well as all the other kinds of headaches that we suffer from today except perhaps "inventory headache." It is even likely that early man suffered more from headache than we who live in the twentieth century because so far as is known no effective treatment for this common problem was available until recently.

Definition.

It is not possible to give a simple definition of migraine that would please even a small number of those who consider themselves authorities in this area. There is little agreement on what migraine really is. Migraine is different things to different people. One could not even begin the definition by calling it a headache since some authorities believe that migraine can in some cases consist of a group of symptoms unassociated with headache. These may include chest pain, abdominal pain, and various visual disturbances. This lack of agreement on a definition of migraine has seriously retarded progress in research into its cause and in finding better treatment for this condition.

An attempt has been made to overcome some of this confusion by classifying migraine into several different types. Along with this effort to simplify and clarify, there has been

MIGRAINE: THERE ARE SEVERAL KINDS

a tendency to include in the migraine group many conditions and types of headaches that probably should not be included at all. For this reason the term has become so broad and non-specific that it really isn't very meaningful.

Classic migraine (migraine with aura).

The best-known kind of migraine is "classic" migraine. This condition usually consists of a severe intermittent headache which is often precipitated by fatigue or emotional stress and which is preceded by a warning. In most cases the warning consists of various abnormalities of vision. The headache is usually located on one side of the head — usually in the temple area and behind and above the eye. Pain usually begins 20 to 30 minutes after the warning starts. The headache can last for variable periods of time — from minutes to days — and is commonly associated with nausea, vomiting, and several other uncomfortable symptoms. The headache is usually of a throbbing, or "vascular," type; but it may also be of a non-throbbing type. Classic migraine is relatively uncommon and makes up less than 10 percent of headaches and other conditions that are usually included in the general category of migraine.

Common migraine (migraine without aura).

The most frequently diagnosed kind of migraine is called "common" migraine. This kind of headache is considered by many to account for nearly half of all headaches that are serious enough to cause the headache patient to seek medical attention. This headache may also be preceded by a warning, as is the case with classic migraine; but in common migraine the warnings are less specific and may not occur at all. These warnings may precede the attack of headache by several hours to several days. They may include irritability, various abdominal symptoms, dizziness, fluid retention, neck muscle contraction, and other uncomfortable sensations. The headache usually lasts longer than that of the classic type; and even though the headache may be located on only one side of the head, it is more frequently located on both sides of the head. The headache is usually thought to be less severe than that which occurs in classic migraine, but severity may vary greatly from one attack to another and from one person to another. The severity of pain of headache is difficult to assess and compare in different individuals. No one can actually state which of two headache sufferers has the more severe headache, but it is likely that each person who has severe headaches thinks his are the worst. Symptoms associated with common migraine are likewise quite variable — including all those which occurred prior to the headache as well as nausea and vomiting, which in some cases can be very severe. Either classic or common migraine can occur at all times of the day, and either of them can cause awakening from sleep.

Other kinds of migraine.

Other kinds of migraine are listed in the classification of headache on page 10. One of these is "cluster headache," which is an uncommon but very severe kind of headache. Still another kind of headache is called "hemiplegic" migraine. It

MIGRAINE: THERE ARE SEVERAL KINDS

gets its name from the associated weakness or paralysis on one side of the body. "Ophthalmoplegic" migraine is characterized by loss of function of some of the muscles that control the eyes. "Lower half" headache refers to headache that is located in the lower part of the face, the cause of which is not known and which is also referred to by several other terms. Other types of "migraine" include basilar artery migraine, abdominal migraine, retinal migraine, cervical migraine, Harris migraine, cardiac migraine, biliary migraine, occlusive migraine, focal migraine, visual migraine, and several other variants,[3] some of which appear to occur only in the mind and eye of the beholder. All of the above variants of migraine, other than classic migraine and common migraine, account for less than one percent of headaches. Still other descriptive terms for headaches that are considered by some to be variants of migraine include the list of miscellaneous situational headaches referred to on page 14. It is erroneously believed by many that all of these "migraine" headaches are due to painful dilation of the blood vessels.

What causes migraine?

The cause of migraine is not known, but emotional stress is the most common precipitating factor.[4] The fact that the cause is not known is understandable and might even be expected when one considers the differences of opinion regarding what migraine actually is and what should be included in this category. For many years migraine has been considered to be a "vascular" headache. Classic migraine was said to be due to abnormal dilation of blood vessels. Some lines of evidence support this view but this idea is being challenged by some.[4] There has never been good evidence that other kinds of migraine are caused by dilation of blood vessels. Pearce cites several references to migraine and the changing theories about its cause from ancient literature up until the present time.[5]

Raskin states that Galen thought "migraine was caused by the dispatch of noxious vapors and fluids from extra cerebral organs, especially the gall bladder."[4] He further states that this widely accepted belief inhibited medical thinking on this subject for the next 1,400 years. When one considers the category of "biliary migraine" which is included in the list from Ryan referred to on page 119, it would seem that little progress has been made even until the present day. In defense of current medical thinking, however, it should be stated that the diagnosis of biliary migraine is probably rarely if ever used by modern physicians. The severe vomiting that can be associated with headache may have accounted for this term and also may have influenced Galen in his beliefs. The causes for migraine and how it can be treated will be considered further in the next three chapters.

References for Chapter 8.

1. Chritchley M. Migraine: from Cappadocia to Queen Square. In: Smith R. Background to migraine – first migraine symposium. New York: Springler-Verlag. 1967:28-38.
2. Ryan RE, Sr, Ryan RE, Jr. Headache and head pain – diagnosis and treatment. St. Louis: The CV Mosby Co, 1978:66.
3. Ryan RE, Sr, Ryan RE, Jr. Headache and head pain – diagnosis and treatment. St. Louis: The CV Mosby Co, 1978:161-175.
4. Raskin NH. Headache. New York: Churchill Livingstone, 1988:35-133.
5. Pearce JMS. Historical aspects of migraine. J. Neurol Neurosurg Psychiatry. 1986;49:1097-1103.

9

Classic Migraine (Migraine With Aura)

Characteristics of classic migraine.

Classic migraine often begins in teenage or early adult life, but it can begin in childhood. Although migraine is not hereditary in a true sense, there seems to be a hereditary predisposition to this condition; so a person is more likely to be affected if other members of his family have it. In those who have migraine, headache occurs with variable frequency from several times a week to one attack in a lifetime. Just as the cause of migraine is not known, all the reasons why some individuals have more frequent attacks than others is not known either, but there are some environmental factors which appear to increase the headache frequency. Emotional stress, anxiety, and anger can precipitate these headaches in some individuals. Certain types of food and beverages may increase the frequency of headache; and in women, migraine is more likely to occur at the time of the menstrual period than at other times of the month.

RELIEF FROM HEADACHE

Migraine attack.

Classic migraine (migraine with aura) is preceded by a warning. The warning can consist of several kinds of symptoms, but it usually affects vision. Commonly occurring warning symptoms vary from loss of vision in half of the visual field of both eyes to isolated blind spots. Other visual warnings consist of zigzag lines, flashes of light, strange figures, and other types of impairment of vision. In some cases the warning consists of tingling sensations or numbness on one side of the body. In occasional cases the visual warnings or other sensory symptoms may occur without headache, but in most cases headache follows the onset of the warning in about twenty to thirty minutes. Although the warning and headache commonly overlap each other for a short period of time, the warnings usually disappear about the time the headache begins. With classic migraine the headache is usually on only one side of the head, but it does not necessarily occur on the same side during each attack. The headache usually has a throbbing quality that is synchronous with the heartbeat. It may last from a few hours to as long as several days, and it varies greatly in severity. Most people find it difficult to carry on normal activity during an attack. Several associated symptoms may occur, such as visual blurring and sensitivity to light; but the most common associated symptoms are nausea and vomiting, which may account for the term "sick headache" which is used by some as a synonym for migraine. In some cases, the "warning" symptoms continue with the headache. These symptoms, as well as the severe headache, often cause the person who has them to seek a dark, quiet place to lie down.

CLASSIC MIGRAINE (MIGRANE WITH AURA)

The cause of migraine.

Although the cause for migraines is not known, traditionally it is believed to be related to an instability of control by the nervous system of the size of blood vessels that carry blood to the head. The aura is thought to be due to abnormal constriction of some of the blood vessels that supply the brain. For this reason parts of the brain do not get enough oxygen and this results in abnormal function of these areas, causing the warning signs. The headache which follows the aura is thought to be due to painful dilation of blood vessels of the scalp, and in some cases vessels supplying the coverings of the brain may also be involved. Evidence for these changes in size of blood vessels comes from several sources. It has been demonstrated that there is a decreased blood flow to the brain during the aura. During the headache there is an increase in the size of some of the blood vessels of the scalp, which can be seen by direct observation. These dilated blood vessels can usually be seen best in the temple region. On the other hand, it can be noted that these blood vessels seem to dilate just as much during heavy exercise or during a hot bath as they do with an attack of migraine; yet headaches do not usually occur in these situations. It has been observed that the severe headache associated with a typical migraine attack can be lessened, and in some cases temporarily relieved, by exerting pressure over the carotid artery or the arteries of the scalp on the affected side of the head to limit blood flow into these vessels. When the carotid artery in the neck is compressed, there is a decrease in blood flow to the brain as well as to the scalp. This procedure is not completely without danger because there have been instances in which cholesterol and other substances from blood vessels affected by hardening of the arteries have come loose when pressure was exerted on these vessels. These loose particles have occasionally caused strokes.

Another line of evidence that suggests that migraine is caused by blood vessel abnormalities is its response to some kinds of chemicals. In the early part of the twentieth century a Swiss chemist named Rothlin found that ergotamine tartrate, a chemical which causes constriction of blood vessels, was successful in treating migraine headache; and this treatment is still known to be effective. Although ergot preparations have several effects on blood vessels and other tissue, one of the most important is that of causing contraction of the muscle tissue in the blood vessel walls, and this causes the blood vessels to get smaller, thus counteracting the painful blood vessel dilation.

It has never been demonstrated with complete certainty that enlargement of the blood vessels associated with classic migraine is the cause of headache, but circumstantial evidence has been supportive of this view. There has been a great deal of research into the cause of the blood vessel abnormalities and pain in migraine, but much of it has been nonproductive. Progress in this area has been slow, and theories have often run far ahead of established fact. Conflicting information has come from different experimental laboratories, and often what appears to be true in one group of migraine patients is not true in another group. This problem is partly due to the failure to agree on which patients should be included in the migraine category because of lack of agreement on a precise defini-

CLASSIC MIGRAINE (MIGRANE WITH AURA)

tion of this condition. Smith appropriately speaks of "the morass of theories which still obscure understanding of the pathogenesis of migraine...."[1] Furthermore, the idea that dilation of blood vessels is the sole cause of migraine is being challenged and most headache authorities no longer believe this to be true.[2]

A current view holds that the symptoms of classic migraine are due chiefly to abnormalities of nerve cells in the brain rather than being due to dilation of blood vessels. Some believe that a slowly spreading depression of function of nerve structures in the brain may be the actual cause of migraine. There are usually some associated blood vessel changes but these may be a secondary phenomenon.

It has been suspected that in at least some individuals with migraine there are changes in the chemicals in the brain during a headache attack. The chemical most often suspected of being related to migraine is the neurotransmitter serotonin. Changes of concentration of this substance in the brain have long been suspected of being related to migraine headache but it has never been determined whether they are cause or effect.

Serotonin dilates some blood vessels and constricts others. During migraine attacks there may be an increase in serotonin excretion in the urine and the level of this substance in the blood decreases. In addition, most of the drugs that are beneficial in the treatment of migraine tend to block the effect of this chemical or enhance its effect. These observations have led to some interesting theories but the actual cause of classic migraine headache continues to be elusive.

RELIEF FROM HEADACHE

One thing seems certain — some individuals have a hereditary predisposition to headache and these persons may develop migraine as well as other types of headache at times and in situations in which those less predisposed have no headache or any other adverse symptoms.

Body chemicals may cause migraine.

There has been extensive research in an effort to find a chemical in the body which causes the blood vessel changes and pain that occur in migraine. Some progress has been made. The observed decrease of serotonin in the blood is associated with an increase in the urine of the substance to which serotonin is metabolized. In addition, it has been found that reserpine, a medicine which can be used in the treatment of high blood pressure and which may in some persons precipitate a headache attack similar to migraine, will also decrease the amount of serotonin in the body. Serotonin is a strong constrictor of some blood vessels, including those in the brain, so decrease of this substance may allow abnormal blood vessel dilation. Against this theory, however, is the observation that serotonin levels do not fall in all migraine patients during an attack. Even though the serotonin level in the blood platelets falls during an attack it has not been demonstrated that plasma serotonin levels are altered enough to cause a change in the size of blood vessels. Several drugs — including Inderal, Elavil, Sansert, and Periactin — that can be used to prevent migraine attacks block the effects of serotonin. Other drugs effective in treating migraine including the triptans seem to increase serotonin effects

CLASSIC MIGRAINE (MIGRANE WITH AURA)

at some neuroreceptors.

Another type of body chemical that may be a factor in causing migraine headache is a group of substances called prostaglandins. These substances were given the name because they were first found in secretion from the prostate gland, but since then they have been found in nearly all tissues of the body. Injection of one type of prostaglandin into persons who have never had migraine previously can produce a typical attack of migraine headache. This same substance also causes dilation of blood vessels. There may be an interaction between prostaglandin and serotonin in causing migraine because it has been shown that serotonin will release prostaglandins from their normal location inside cells into the tissue fluid where they can cause blood vessels to dilate. There is further evidence that prostaglandins may be the cause of painful blood vessel dilation in migraine headache. Several drugs, including aspirin and ergotrate (which are used in the treatment of migraine headaches), counteract the effect of prostaglandins. Several other body chemicals have been suspected of causing migraine headache, but evidence that they actually do this is rather poor so they will not be discussed.

Some foods may cause migraine.

Some kinds of food may cause headache attacks in migraine patients, but this is a rather uncommon occurrence. Foods in this category include strong cheeses, sardines, chocolate, dairy products, citrus fruits, and also alcoholic beverages. It has been suspected by some

RELIEF FROM HEADACHE

that this is on the basis of food allergy, but best available evidence is against this theory. The importance of food allergy as a cause of headache has been exaggerated by some headache specialists. It is more likely that the effect of these migraine-producing foods is due to the presence of certain chemicals in these foods to which susceptible individuals are sensitive. One of these chemicals is tyramine. Tyramine is similar chemically to epinephrine (adrenaline). It is capable of increasing blood pressure, and in some individuals it can produce severe headache; but this certainly is not the explanation for migraine attacks in the majority of individuals who suffer from this condition.

Chinese food causes headache in some people. It contains liberal amounts of monosodium glutamate and this appears to be the cause of the headache. This substance also causes Chinese restaurant syndrome, which consists of headache and several other uncomfortable symptoms. But these symptoms occur only in some susceptible individuals. It has been demonstrated that pyridoxine (vitamin B_6) taken by mouth can reduce or prevent headache and other symptoms caused by monosodium glutamate.[3]

Other foods that may precipitate attacks of migraine and which may also cause other kinds of headache in susceptible individuals include preserved meats such as hot dogs, sandwich meats, and bologna. These "hot dog" headaches are caused by chemical preservatives called nitrites and nitrates that are used in these meats.

Exposure to nitrites and nitrates may occur from other sources. Nitroglycerin, which is also a nitrate, and

CLASSIC MIGRAINE (MIGRANE WITH AURA)

similar substances that are used to dilate coronary blood vessels in individuals who have coronary artery disease of the heart will produce a similar kind of headache. Still another situation in which this kind of chemical can cause headache is that in which there is exposure to explosives. There is some difference of opinion as to whether these headaches should be considered to be migraine headaches, but it appears that individuals who have migraine are quite susceptible to headaches caused by nitrites and nitrates, and in some cases these substances produce migraine attacks.

Emotions and migraine.

There is a relationship between psychological factors and frequency of attacks of migraine, but psychological factors and emotional stress appear to have little if anything to do with the primary cause of this condition. Many individuals who have migraine observe that they are much more likely to get an attack if they are under emotional pressure or if they are unusually fatigued. But these same individuals may have attacks of migraine at other times when there is no recognized emotional stress. Psychological profiles of patients have suggested that the typical migraine patient is more intelligent and is a higher achiever than his associates who do not have this condition. Some of these studies also suggest that persons with migraine are rigid, perfectionists, compulsive, and anxious with suppressed hostility and inability to express anger. It has been stated, "As a rule, migraine sufferers have a superiority complex."[4] More recent studies have shown, however, that there is no personality type characteristic of migraine,[2] and the less affluent and the less intelligent are also troubled by this problem. These opinions about personality types, social position, and intelligence of patients subject to migraine now appear to be more a reflection of the type of patients to which certain headache authorities limited their practice rather than to characteristics of the entire migraine population.

Hormones and headache.

Changes in hormone levels often produce headaches in women who are subject to migraine. About half the women who have migraine experience more headaches during or near the time of their menstrual period than during the rest of the cycle. Pregnancy also changes headache pattern. Many individuals who have migraine get relief from this condition during pregnancy, but a few women have more severe headaches during that time. Oral contraceptives increase the frequency of headache in some women and the headache frequency appears to correlate best with the estrogen, or female hormone, content of the oral contraceptive. This, however, is not always true because a few women with migraine report that their headaches improve when they take oral contraceptives. The inconsistencies that occur in the relationship between hormones and headache, like the inconsistency in other factors related to migraine, show how complicated this condition is and how difficult it is to arrive at an acceptable theory about its cause that fits all cases.

CLASSIC MIGRAINE (MIGRANE WITH AURA)

Family history.

Studies of the families of patients who suffer from migraine suggest that there is a family history for this condition in over 50 percent of cases. This is especially true of childhood migraine, which is defined as migraine occurring before ten years of age. Some of these family histories may be misleading, however, because of the lack of precision of definition and diagnosis of migraine. A false positive family history for migraine may be obtained in some cases because this condition has often been over-diagnosed. Since headache is such a common condition, it is a rare family that does not have some members with this problem; and, therefore, a family history of migraine is easy to obtain but not always correct. A family history of headache does not necessarily mean that the headache is hereditary. Other factors, including emotional problems in the family, may be the cause of this problem. It has been said that in some families, headache becomes a way of life and a means of coping in a stressful environment. Headache may be more common in members of a family in which there are constant domestic problems even if no hereditary factor is present.

Blood vessel abnormalities.

No abnormalities of blood vessels or other tissues that can be demonstrated by microscopic examination are characteristically present in patients with migraine. In migraine attacks of long duration there may be some changes in the blood vessel walls, including fluid accumulation and possibly some mild inflammatory change. These changes may account for some stiffening and thickness of the blood vessel walls, which makes the headaches more difficult to treat; but no microscopic abnormalities that appear to relate to the cause of the headache has been found.

Occasionally the changes in blood vessels occurring with an attack of migraine are so severe that a stroke with permanent brain damage and impairment of physical function results. These abnormalities may include paralysis on one side of the body, impairment of sensation on one side, or permanent visual abnormality. Figure 1 shows a CT scan from such a case. This CT scan shows evidence of a stroke which occurred in an otherwise healthy, forty-two year old male who had the stroke during a severe migraine attack.

Treatment of migraine.

Migraine can usually be successfully treated if the diagnosis is correct. The most effective drugs at present for treatment of an acute attack of migraine are the triptans. These drugs act at receptor sites in the brain. The first one on the market was sumatriptan (Imitrex). There are several similar drugs marketed by other companies. These include rizatriptan (Maxalt), zolmitriptan (Zomig) and several others. These medications are effective for aborting attacks of migraine or treating the migraine attack after it has developed and are usually effective for several hours. Around 60 to 75 percent of persons are

CLASSIC MIGRAINE (MIGRANE WITH AURA)

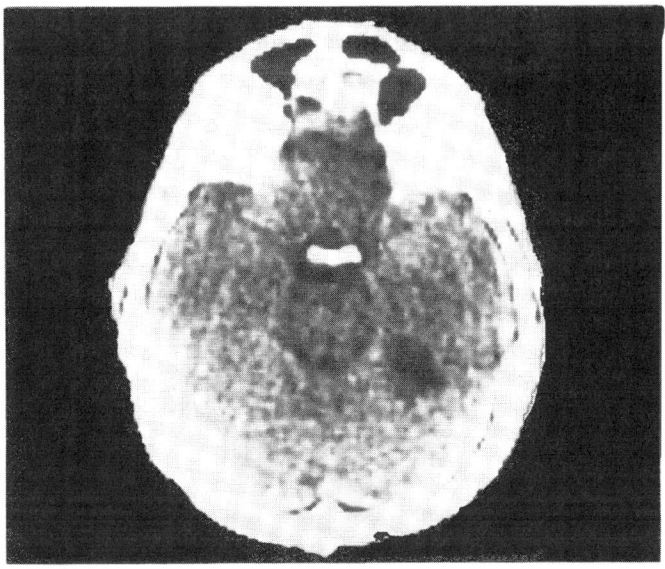

Figure 1. Computed tomogram (CT scan) showing a cerebral infarction (stroke) which occurred during a migraine attack. There was slow recovery over a one-year period, but some permanent impairment of function remained. The dark area on the right side near the midline is the area of infarction.

successfully treated by these medications but their use is limited in some persons by side effects, especially in older persons. There have been a few cases of strokes and heart attacks associated with the use of these medications. More common side effects include strange sensations such as tingling and burning, heaviness and pressure in the chest, mental confusion and others. These drugs are usually taken by mouth but for those persons who cannot tolerate oral medications during a migraine attack because of the associated nausea and vomiting some of them are available by injection or nasal spray. These medications are available by prescription only.

Prior to the newer and more effective drugs for treatment of migraine, some of the more effective medications were preparations containing ergot which have been used for many years. These drugs have an interesting history and long before it was known that they were effective for treatment of headache there was knowledge of some of their toxic effects.

Ergot compounds can be obtained from a fungus that infests some grains, including wheat and rye. This poisonous fungus grows especially well in a warm moist climate. In the middle ages there were outbreaks of a severe disease called St. Anthony's fire, which was caused by eating grain that was infested with this substance.[5] The abnormalities consisted chiefly of gangrene of the extremities, nausea, and vomiting. The gangrene caused loss of fingers, toes, and sometimes an entire extremity, and in a few cases destruction of internal organs from lack of blood supply. This lack of blood supply and the resulting gangrene were caused by severe constriction of blood vessels that supplied these organs and extremities. This condition was called St. Anthony's fire because the affected extremities turned black with gangrene and looked as if they had been burned. Outbreaks of this condition are reported to have occurred commonly in some warm, humid areas of southern France; but they also occurred throughout the world, even in the United States. St. Anthony's fire could be treated by going to St. Anthony's shrine where food was

CLASSIC MIGRAINE (MIGRANE WITH AURA)

less likely to be contaminated by fungus-infested grain because it was less wet and humid there. Ergot-infested food also caused pregnant women to lose their babies by abortion or miscarriage because it caused the uterus to contract and expel the incompletely developed baby prematurely.

Ergot compounds are most effective for migraine if they are taken while the aura or warning is still present and before the headache begins. The direct effect of these compounds on the smooth muscle in the walls of the blood vessels causes the blood vessels to constrict and thus prevent the abnormal, painful dilation of these blood vessels. However, they may also produce their anti-migraine effect by other mechanisms. This medication is less effective after headache begins, but it can be helpful to some degree during the headache.

Ergot can be taken in several different forms. One of the most popular is a combination of ergotamine (a purified form of ergot) and caffeine, known as Cafergot. The caffeine given with the ergot helps treat the headache and also increases absorption of ergot from the stomach and the intestine. To be most effective, Cafergot tablets should be taken in a dosage of one or two tablets as soon as the visual disturbance or other warning signs begin, and then one tablet every twenty to thirty minutes if the headache develops. To prevent toxicity, however, no more than six tablets should be taken during one headache attack and no more than eight or ten tablets should be used in one week. Unfortunately many individuals develop nausea and vomiting when they have a migraine attack, so it is difficult for them to hold the medication in their stomach.

RELIEF FROM HEADACHE

Because of the possible danger involved in the use of all ergot drugs these substances are available by prescription only. In addition to the serious toxic effects mentioned above, other toxic effects of ergot compounds include abdominal cramps, abnormalities of sensation, confusion, and convulsions. If liver disease, infection, or hardening of the arteries are present, complications are more likely to occur than in healthy individuals. If coronary artery disease is present heart attacks may be precipitated by these drugs. Ergot preparations should not be used during pregnancy.

There is another danger in the use of ergot if it is used frequently. It can produce drug dependence. If persons with chronic headache get good relief from this drug, they may take it in excessive amounts. When ergot is taken daily, a state of dependence often develops in which a severe headache occurs every time the effect of the drug wears off. This severe headache is readily relieved by taking additional medication. When ergot dependence is present, severe withdrawal headaches and other withdrawal symptoms may occur for a period of several days to a week when this drug is discontinued.

Several other drugs can be helpful in treating an acute attack of migraine. One such drug is Midrin. This medication contains a vasoconstrictor and an analgesic but no ergot. Although Midrin is usually less effective than ergot containing compounds it may be helpful in individuals who do not tolerate ergot. Simple analgesics such as aspirin, Anacin, Excedrin, Advil, and Tylenol may be of some benefit. In some individuals, headache may be so severe and persistent that narcotic analgesics

CLASSIC MIGRAINE (MIGRANE WITH AURA)

such as codeine, Darvon, Talwin, or Demerol are needed for the acute attack. All of these compounds may cause drug dependence in addition so they should be used with caution. Some migraine patients become very resistant to treatment and cannot get relief from some of their attacks unless they take combinations of medications — including injections of narcotics such as Demerol, along with tranquilizers such as Vistaril, and sedative drugs such as Valium — in sufficient dosage so they can go to sleep for several hours. This combination of drugs usually stops the migraine attack.

Caffeine taken in the form of a cup of strong coffee or one or two bottles of Coca-Cola along with two aspirin tablets can prevent migraine attacks in some persons if these substances are taken when the warning of the attack first begins.

If persons with migraine have less than one attack every two weeks, treatment of the acute attack by the methods mentioned above is usually the most satisfactory management. For individuals who have more frequent attacks and for those who are incapacitated for several days during each attack, preventive treatment is often more satisfactory.

Some medications are effective for prevention of migraine. These include some of the antiepileptic drugs, methysergide (Sansert), amitriptyline (Elavil), propranolol (Inderal), and others. All of these drugs are obtained by prescription only and should be used under the direction of a physician because they all have potential for serious toxicity.

Of the antiepileptic drugs used for treatment of headache, one of the most effective is divalproex (Depakote). This drug may cause several uncomfortable side effects including nausea and vomiting, drowsiness, tremor, dizziness, itching and transient hair loss. There have been a few fatalities due to this drug's toxic effect on the liver but this is very rare.

Another antiepileptic drug that has been used with some success for prevention of migraine is gabapentin (Neurontin). This drug also has some uncomfortable side effects in some people including somnolence, dizziness, unsteadiness, tremor, nervousness and other symptoms but serious side effects are uncommon. Other antiepileptic drugs have been used for treatment of headache. Some of them are very expensive

Sansert has a chemical structure similar to that of ergot compounds, and its chemical structure is also similar to that of LSD. One of its effects is to antagonize the effect of serotonin in the body, but this may not necessarily be the means by which it prevents migraine. Side effects include nausea, abdominal cramps, strange sensations in the abdomen, and occasionally hallucinations. The most serious side effect is obstruction of flow of urine from the kidneys to the bladder and obstruction of some kinds of blood vessels, but this rarely if ever occurs if the drug is taken in proper dosage and for less than six months. For this reason the drug should be discontinued for a one-month drug holiday at least every six months.

Elavil is an antidepressant drug, but its effect in the prevention of migraine appears to be in addition to and probably separate from its effect in treatment of depression. This drug may produce drowsiness, dizziness, loss

CLASSIC MIGRAINE (MIGRANE WITH AURA)

of balance, dry mouth and various other uncomfortable symptoms. Serious side effects are uncommon.

Inderal is a drug that is used in treatment of hypertension and some kinds of heart disease. Its beneficial effect in prevention of migraine may be due to its ability to stabilize blood vessels, making them less likely to abnormally constrict and dilate. Side effects may include drowsiness, depression, weakness, and lightheadedness. This drug can make congestive heart failure or asthma worse, so it should not be used when these conditions are present. Inderal has antianxiety action which may account for some of its beneficial effect against migraine.

Nonsteroidal antiinflammatory drugs including Naproxyn, Clinoril, Motrin, and several others may be helpful for some people.[6] Most of these drugs can cause side effects. They may cause irritation of the stomach resulting in peptic ulcer which can cause hemorrhage and other complications. In some respects these drugs are like aspirin which is also classified as a nonsteroidal antiinflammatory drug.

Calcium channel blocking drugs such as Verapamil (Calan), Niphedipine (Procardia), Nimodipine (Ninotop) and others seem to help a few people with severe headaches. There will probably be no end of "new" antiheadache medications. Unfortunately most of them provide symptomatic treatment only and do not get rid of the cause of the headache.

Other drugs may be helpful in some cases. Oxygen inhalation described in chapter 11 for treatment of cluster headache may be helpful for aborting the acute migraine attack. Cyproheptadine (Periactin) is an antihistamine drug that also counteracts the effect of serotonin. It has been reported to be effective in some cases for prevention of migraine. Low-dosage ergot tablets used daily have also decreased the severity and frequency of migraine in some individuals. Many other drugs have been used, but they are usually not very effective and some of them are no more effective than a placebo.

Change in lifestyle may help prevent migraine.

A change in diet and lifestyle may be just as important in prevention of migraine as is the use of drugs. Although no specific type of lifestyle would prevent migraine in all individuals, and there are no specific prohibitions for migraine sufferers, general healthful living practices can be helpful in most cases. Since stress and emotional disturbances tend to increase migraine headache frequency, these factors should be decreased as much as possible. In some cases this may require counseling; but in general, psychotherapy for migraine has not been very effective. Good health measures, such as getting adequate exercise and rest, are important. Exercise should be vigorous enough and prolonged enough to produce mild fatigue. If this occurs, relaxation and the ability to get adequate sleep without medication usually results; and it is then easier to cope with the normal stresses of everyday life. Solomon, who is reputed to be the wisest man who ever lived, is thought by some to have said in Ecclesiastes 5:12, "The sleep of a laboring man is sweet. . . ." Physical activity is still one of the best prescriptions for relaxation and sleep that is known today.

CLASSIC MIGRAINE (MIGRANE WITH AURA)

Specific food sensitivities and intolerances do not appear to be a factor for most people with migraine headache, but in a few individuals some types of food or beverage may precipitate attacks. A trial period of eliminating certain foods from the diet is worthwhile. The substances that have been reported to most commonly precipitate headaches in susceptible individuals include alcoholic beverages, chocolate, strong cheese, some kinds of fish, dairy products, citrus fruits, preserved meats and food containing monosodium glutamate; but nearly any kind of food substance can precipitate migraine in an occasional individual. A regular balanced diet consisting of healthful food may be of more importance for most individuals than eliminating any specific type of food substance from the diet.

If migraine headaches begin or become worse or more frequent with the use of birth control medications, these medications should be discontinued. Persons who have headaches who use these drugs should stop taking them for a trial period even if they have not observed a relationship between their headaches and the use of these substances.

Non-medical treatment.

Several types of physical and electrical measures have been beneficial in preventing migraine as well as other kinds of headaches in a few individuals. Some have gotten help by manipulation done by chiropractors, which in some cases may facilitate muscle relaxation. Others have received benefit from acupuncture or acupressure techniques done in various ways. Hypnosis and yoga, as well as various forms of medication and relaxation techniques, have all been utilized; each one has its advocates. However, there are no good controlled studies of any of these measures that show they are very effective. It can be stated in general that anything that provides exercise and assists in muscle relaxation can be beneficial in some cases.

One of the currently popular means of treating migraine by physical measures is the use of biofeedback training. Biofeedback training is a means of teaching an individual to control certain previously involuntary and reflex body activities by monitoring body function with electrical instruments. By observing the measurements of body function seen in the electrical instrument, a person can often learn by experimentation how to exert control over some of these functions. For example, it is possible to learn to have partial control over such body functions as blood pressure, pulse rate, temperature and even some types of brain wave patterns. Muscle relaxation can also be learned by this method. Techniques which teach control over circulation in the hand to produce hand warming and also those which teach scalp and neck muscle relaxation have been found to be beneficial in treatment of some migraine patients. Although some investigators have given glowing reports of their successes in treatment of migraine by this means, most research studies reveal that this treatment of migraine is not very effective.

CLASSIC MIGRAINE (MIGRANE WITH AURA)

References for Chapter 9.

1. Smith LH, Jr. Foreword in Raskin NH, Appenzeller O. Headache. Vol XIX in the series: Major problems in internal medicine. Philadelphia: WB Saunders Co, 1980:V.
2. Raskin NH. Headache. New York: Churchill Livingstone 1988:35-133.
3. Folkers K. Shizukuishi S, Scudder SL, et al. Biochemical evidence for a deficiency of vitamin B_6 in subjects reacting to monosodium L-glutamate by Chinese restaurant syndrome. Biochem Biophs Res Commun 1981;100:972-977.
4. Ryan, RE, Sr, Ryan RE, Jr. Headache and head pain — diagnosis and treatment. St. Louis: The CV Mosby Co, 1978:67.
5. Brazenu P. Drugs affecting uterine motility. In: Goodman LS, Gilman A, eds. The pharmacological basis of therapeutics. 5th ed. New York; Macmillan Publishing Co, Inc, 1970:872.
6. Peterson DI. Headache: Part IX–Nonsteroidal antiinflammatory drugs for the treatment of headache. IM 1986;7:69-77.

10

Common Migraine
(Migraine Without Aura)

What is common migraine?

The definition of common migraine in some ways is relatively easy because almost any headache can qualify. It is usually defined as a vascular headache which may or may not have warning symptoms. If warning symptoms are present they are usually rather vague and consist of mood changes, fluid retention, insomnia, thirst, hunger, and various other discomforts which are not uncommon in usual human experience of most people. In the period of warning, there are no actual impairments of brain function like those that occur in classic migraine. The headache usually begins gradually; it can be on either one side of the head or both sides; it may be throbbing or nonthrobbing; and it is often associated with nausea, vomiting, sensitivity to light, irritability, increase in flow of tears and nasal secretions, and various other symptoms. The headache may last for variable periods of time, from a few hours to many days. Some believe common migraine attacks are more severe than muscle-contraction headaches, but this cannot be proven.

COMMON MIRAINE (MIGRAINE WITHOUT AURA)

Evidence that common migraine is caused by changes in size and sensitivity of blood vessels is less convincing than it is in the case of classic migraine. The fact that the headache of common migraine is often throbbing in type suggests that it has a vascular cause. But throbbing is not always present; and furthermore, "throbbing" also occurs with muscle-contraction or tension headache. Many patients who are diagnosed as having common migraine state that they have throbbing headaches on some occasions and nonthrobbing headaches on other occasions. Although ergot preparations and other medications that affect blood vessels are less helpful in treatment of common migraine (migraine without aura) than they are for classic migraine, they may produce a favorable response. This suggests that dilation of blood vessels may be at least partially responsible for the headache. Relief of headache by ergot preparations, however, does not establish a vascular cause. Many years ago Barrie and associates found that responsiveness to ergotamine correlated better with the severity of headache than with the criteria for migraine.[1] Horton and associates found that tension headache as well as migraine responded well to a mixture of ergot and caffeine.[2] Triptans may be very helpful in some persons who have migraine without aura.

Common migraine and tension headache are similar.

Most of the information gained by research about the relationship of dilation of blood vessels and headache concerns classic migraine, and even some of that is controversial. There is no good evidence that common migraine is caused by blood vessel abnormalities. Olesen and associates found no change in blood flow in the brain before common migraine attacks. For this reason they suggest that common migraine and classic migraine may be caused by different mechanisms.[3] Furthermore, the relationship of the effects of body chemicals, such as serotonin and prostaglandins, to common migraine is chiefly by inference because of the belief that common migraine is similar to classic migraine. It appears that the traditional belief that common migraine is due to a vascular etiology and the tendency to mix classic and common migraine has been incorrect and at least partially responsible for the lack of progress in getting a better understanding of migraine. Common migraine may be more like tension headache than it is like classic migraine. The practice of lumping "common migraine" and "classic migraine" together and believing both of them to be due to blood vessel abnormalities, and then separating common migraine from muscle-contraction headache and considering them to be distinct entities now appears to be unjustified.

The following report shows how similar muscle-contraction headache and common migraine are. Bakal and Kaganov[4] found that 40 percent of patients with migraine and also 40 percent of patients with tension or muscle-contraction headache reported having throbbing-type headaches. Fifty percent of patients from each group reported having visual disturbances associated with the headache and 50 percent of each group reported that there were family members who also suffered from headache. Seventy percent of the patients diagnosed as migraine had nausea and vomiting and 35 percent of the patients with tension headache experienced nausea and vomiting. Inderol and other beta blockers can be beneficial in treating some patients with

COMMON MIRAINE (MIGRAINE WITHOUT AURA)

each kind of headache. Many individuals who have a diagnosis of common migraine have painful, sustained neck muscle contraction similar to that of persons with muscle-contraction headache. Electrical studies to compare contractions of neck muscles in patients with a diagnosis of migraine and in those with a diagnosis of muscle-contraction headache reveal that there is as much muscle tension in the migraine patients as there is in the patients with the diagnosis of muscle-contraction or tension headache.[5] Painful sustained contraction of neck muscles is an important factor in the cause of headaches in many persons who have a diagnosis of common migraine; but this important factor has often been ignored because of the emphasis that has been placed on the vascular component of common migraine.

Several investigators have concluded that abnormalities in the neck and in the region of the junction between the head and neck can cause headache. Furthermore, the characteristics of these headaches can be the same as those used for the diagnosis of common migraine.[6] In addition, many patients with a diagnosis of common migraine respond successfully to neck mobilization therapy described in Chapter 2. These observations cast serious doubt on the concept that "common migraine" is usually caused by abnormalities of blood vessels — a belief that has been entrenched in the thinking of physicians for over fifty years.

Treatment.

Common migraine can be treated with some success with the same drugs and physical methods that are used in management of classic migraine, but the treatment is often

RELIEF FROM HEADACHE

less effective. Triptans including Imitrex, Zomig, and Maxalt are very helpful for some persons. In acute attacks, analgesics are often helpful. These include aspirin, Tylenol, Advil, and other pain-killing drugs. When the headache is severe, Demerol or some other injectable narcotic analgesic medication may be necessary to obtain relief. Tranquilizers such as Librium, Valium, and several similar drugs may also be helpful. If these medications are used frequently, they present a danger of drug dependence.

Traditional preventive treatment for common migraine is similar to that used in the treatment of classic migraine. Antidepressants such as Elavil may be helpful in some cases. Inderal is also effective in some cases, and occasionally Sansert or small dosages of ergot given on a regular daily basis may prevent attacks. Midrin may also be effective, but none of these drugs can be considered to be a great success in treatment or prevention of most cases of common migraine. Physical methods such as biofeedback, acupuncture, relaxation therapy, and various exercise programs may also be of some benefit. Headaches that occur at least fifteen days each month are called chronic daily headaches. These usually respond well to the treatment described in chapter two.

In general, common migraine is poorly treated by traditional methods. Management of patients with these headaches usually consists chiefly of tests to rule out serious diseases such as brain tumors and other intracranial pathology and use of Inderal, Elavil, tranquilizers and pain-killing medications for symptomatic relief. If x-rays and other tests show no evidence of serious disease and if the patient does not respond to traditional and usually somewhat ineffective medical treatment, he is often told he will have to "learn to

COMMON MIRAINE (MIGRAINE WITHOUT AURA)

live with your headaches." Many people with a diagnosis of common migraine suffer from headaches for many years without finding any effective treatment.

In most cases it is not necessary to continue to suffer from these headaches and keep on taking pain-killing medication. It has been demonstrated that most persons with chronic headaches, including those diagnosed as common migraine as well as those diagnosed as muscle-contraction headache, can get good relief from headache by the simple measures described in chapter 2.

References for Chapter 10.

1. Barrie MA, Fox WR, Weatherall M, et al. Analysis of symptoms of patients with headaches and their response to treatment with ergot derivatives. Quart J Med 1968;37:319-336.
2. Horton BT, Ryan R. Reynolds JL. Clinical observations on the use of E.C. 110, a new agent for the treatment of headache. Mayo Clin Proc 1948;23:105-108.
3. Olesen J, Tfelt-Hansen P, Hendricksen L, Larsen B. The common migraine attack may not be initiated by cerebral ischemia. Lancet 1981;2:438-440.
4. Bakal DA, Kaganov JA. Muscle contraction and migraine headache: Psycho physiologic comparison. Headache 1977;17:208-215.
5. Pozniak-Patewicz E. "Cephalgic" spasm of head and neck muscles. Headache 1976;14:261-266.
6. Edmeads J. The cervical spine and headache. Neurology 1985;38:1874-1878,.

11

Cluster Headache and Other Uncommon Forms of Head Pain

Cluster headache.

Cluster headache is a distinctive type of headache that is usually considered to be a variant of migraine. It is much less frequent than migraine, but occasionally one individual may have both kinds of headache. One of the characteristics of cluster headache is its severity. It is so severe that many affected persons consider committing suicide during their headache attacks. Fortunately the attacks do not last very long. The usual duration is from ten minutes to two hours, and a large percentage of cases last less than one hour. Cluster headache comes on suddenly without warning. It is always unilateral and during each "cluster" it is always located on the same side of the head or even in some instances on one side of the face. It rarely if ever affects the back part of the head. It is usually nonthrobbing in type and has some characteristic associated symptoms. One of the symptoms is tearing from the eye on the same side of the head on which the headache is located. Stuffiness of the nose on the side

CLUSTER HEADACHE

of the headache may also be present. In some cases there is irritation and redness of the eye, and there may even be redness of the face on the side of the headache. In about 20 percent of cases the pupil of the eye gets small and the eyelid droops (Horner's syndrome) on the side of the headache. The headache may go away almost as abruptly as it came on, but on some occasions it may regress slowly.

This kind of headache is called cluster headache because it occurs in clusters of attacks which have a frequency of two to three per week to as often as several a day. These recurrent headaches may continue for a period of a few weeks to as long as several months, after which time there is usually a headache-free period for several weeks to several years. In a few instances the headaches keep recurring frequently for as long as several years without any headache-free periods. A large proportion of headache attacks occur at night; and cluster headache is one of the conditions — in addition to intracranial hemorrhage, meningitis, brain tumor, cervical spine disease, and glaucoma — which characteristically awakens a person from a sound sleep with excruciating headache. Cluster headache is considered to be a variant of migraine because it can be treated with some of the same drugs that are used for the treatment of migraine. There also may be dilation of blood vessels in cluster headache attacks just as there is in migraine.

Some substances, such as alcohol and nitroglycerin which dilate blood vessels, have a tendency to precipitate cluster headache. At one time, it was believed that cluster headaches were precipitated by an excessive amount of histamine in the blood stream, so it was called histamine headache. But the actual cause of the headache is not known, and it is no longer believed to be due to histamine. Psychogenic and emotional factors usually do not seem to be significant in the production of cluster headache. It is uncommon to find two members of one family with this condition so it does not appear to be hereditary.

As in the case of migraine, the acute attack of cluster headache can be treated with triptans or ergot preparations with some success, but no treatment which depends on a symptomatic treatment of each individual attack is very effective. This is true because cluster headache attacks are very severe, they come on very rapidly, and usually last for a relatively short period of time. So there is not sufficient time for the drug to be absorbed and take effect. For these reasons prevention is the best treatment. Treatment to prevent attacks of cluster headache is usually successful, and several drugs are effective for this purpose. It has been learned only in the last few years that lithium carbonate, a drug that is often used to treat manic states in manic depressive psychosis, is also effective in preventing attacks of cluster headache. The same can be said for steroids such as prednisone, a synthetic drug that is like cortisone in action. This drug can be used to prevent cluster headache, but it is ineffective for acute attacks. Serious side effects can occur from either one of these drugs if they are not used according to instructions.

The drug that has been used most extensively in prevention of cluster headache and which is effective in at least 60 to 70 percent of cases is methysergide (Sansert). This is one of the drugs that can also be used to prevent migraine attacks. It is closely related chemically to the ergot compounds. Unfortunately Sansert does have some serious side effects, especially if it is taken for a period longer than six months. One of these side effects has to do with formation of scar tissue around the kidneys and ureters, with obstruction of urine flow from the kidneys. If a one-month drug holiday is taken every six months, during which time no Sansert is used, this complication rarely occurs. There are, however, some uncomfortable symptoms that frequently result from this medication. These consist of abnormal sensations in the abdomen and extremities, abdominal pain and muscle cramps, dizziness, feeling of pins and needles in the extremities, impairment of vision, and, in some cases, confusion and a strange sense of unreality. Nevertheless, by careful adjustment of dosage, most people can use this medication very satisfactorily.

Other drugs including calcium channel blockers, cyproheptadine (Periactin), small doses of ergotamine tartrate used each day, and the use of analgesics of several types have been less successful. All of the drugs that are commonly used in the treatment or prevention of cluster headaches are prescription drugs.

Another type of treatment that can be helpful in the acute attack of cluster headache and which is effective in about 50 percent of cases is inhalation of 100 percent oxygen at a rate of eight liters per minute for a period of fifteen to twenty minutes. A few individuals with cluster headache have found that vigorous exercise immediately after its onset will abort the attack. In some cases an attack can be avoided by putting a local anesthetic solution in the back part of the nose. Cluster headache is serious only because of the severe pain that it causes. There is no evidence that it produces any specific damage to the body; nor is it due to any serious disease.

A variant of cluster headache called paroxsysmal

hemicrania can be successfully treated with indomethacin (Indocin). This headache differs from cluster headache in that attacks are shorter in duration and may occur many times each day.

Hemiplegic and ophthalmoplegic types of migraine.

Hemiplegic migraine is characterized by weakness or paralysis of one side of the body associated with a migraine attack. In some cases the weakness or paralysis of one side is the warning that occurs before the headache begins. In these cases the abnormality of function usually resolves within twenty or thirty minutes just as do visual disturbances that precede classic migraine attacks. These cases of migraine are similar to classic migraine except that the focal neurological symptoms that occur before the headache arise from a different part of the brain. In some cases of hemiplegic migraine, weakness or paralysis of one side of the body is also present during the headache and may even last for days to several weeks after the headache goes away. Other abnormalities — including loss of sensation, loss of ability to speak, and incoordination — may occur associated with the weakness or paralysis. Hemiplegic migraine is a rare condition; even in individuals who have this problem attacks are usually infrequent. In some cases several members of a family are affected, so it appears to be hereditary. Hemiplegic migraine usually begins in childhood.

Ophthalmoplegic migraine is similar to hemiplegic migraine, except that the abnormality of function involves the muscles that move the eyes. It causes partial or complete paralysis of function of these muscles, resulting in double vision. In some cases, impairment of function of eye muscles has lasted for several months.

Migraine of either hemiplegic or ophthalmoplegic type, as well as other kinds in which the aura (or warning) consists of neurological abnormalities other than visual disturbances, may be referred to as "complicated" migraine. The abnormalities may be permanent in some cases. The most important concern in these types of migraine is the question of whether some other and more serious abnormality, such as brain tumor or intracranial aneurysm, is present. For this reason extensive examination and x-ray testing with CT scanning or MRI scanning and in some cases angiography may be necessary to rule out serious disease before these diagnoses can be made with confidence.

Treatment of these rare forms of migraine is poorly understood, but in some cases they seem to respond to the same types of treatment used for classic migraine. It is likely that the neurological abnormalities in these conditions are due to severe constriction of the arteries of the brain, causing decrease in blood flow to some portions of the brain. For this reason there has been some reluctance to use vasoconstrictor drugs, such as the ergot preparations, for treatment since these drugs could possibly make the abnormality worse. There is no good evidence at present that this is true; nevertheless, this possibility still needs to be considered. It is likely that some cases that have been diagnosed as hemiplegic migraine have been cases in which an unrecognized stroke occurred during a migraine attack. There are well-documented cases, however, in which there have been several attacks of hemiplegic migraine; and yet, no evidence of permanent impairment of brain function or stroke could be found. The use of Inderol is believed by some to be dangerous in hemiplegic migraine and the use of triptans is not advisable.

Lower-half headache.

Lower-half headache is even more uncommon and less well understood than the other variants of migraine mentioned above. It consists of severe pain in the lower half of the face, the specific cause of which has not been found. In some cases, otolaryngologists have reported that surgery on the nose to correct abnormalities of the nasal septum or drainage of infection from an infected sphenoid sinus relieves the symptoms. These procedures seem to be effective in only a few cases so the treatment of this condition by this means is often not successful. Precision of definition and diagnosis of this kind of head pain presents some problems, and this condition may actually include several different entities. How this condition came to be classified as a form of migraine is a legitimate question.

12

Headache Associated with Mental Illness

Not all "psychogenic" headaches are due to mental illness.

Mental illness can cause headache as well as other kinds of pain but most "psychogenic headaches" are not caused by mental illness. It is not uncommon for ordinary muscle-contraction headaches to be precipitated or aggravated by the common everyday stresses of life. These include anxiety, anger, and frustration that can be experienced by anyone. These headaches may be referred to incorrectly as psychogenic headaches by some physicians. This type of headache should not be confused with headache due to psychosis or mental illness. Muscle-contraction or myofascial headaches, some of which are due to emotional stress, are very common and are experienced by most people at some time in their life. In some studies of the various causes of headache, it has been found that over 50 percent of persons who have headaches severe enough to cause them to seek medical attention have this kind of headache.

Even though some physicians use the term psycho-

RELIEF FROM HEADACHE

genic headache as a synonym for muscle-contraction headache, it would be inappropriate to consider this large group of people with muscle-contraction headache mentally ill and to believe that their headaches are due to mental illness. Mental illness should not be considered to be the cause of headache unless there is some evidence in the patient's behavior or in his thought patterns that is consistent with such a diagnosis. Even then, all other causes of headaches should also be considered. Some physicians, however, assume inappropriately that anyone who complains of pain or headache either imagines his symptoms or has some emotional instability if he does not have serious organic diseases such as a tumor, hemorrhage, or infection, and if he does not have migraine.

It is not uncommon for physicians, especially in a hospital setting, to attribute patient complaints to emotional disturbances if the cause of the pain or other symptoms cannot be demonstrated by some laboratory or x-ray test. This kind of thinking often carries over into physicians' views of patients with headache in which no serious disease can be found. Patients who can be given a diagnosis of "migraine," however, are believed to have legitimate headaches because it is thought that these headaches are due to abnormalities of blood vessels. On the other hand, persons with muscle-contraction or tension headache are considered by some physicians to have headaches on a psychogenic basis because they do not have blood vessel abnormalities or any abnormal x-rays or blood tests. All this is in spite of the fact that it has been demonstrated that there is no clear-cut difference between common migraine and muscle-contraction headache. Both are associated with tight painful neck

HEADACHE ASSOCIATED WITH MENTAL ILLNESS

muscles. Emotional stress or tension may trigger either one, and both respond to the same kinds of treatment.

What causes pain?

Some headaches actually are due to mental illness. Initially it may be difficult to understand how this could be so, but a better comprehension of what pain consists of will make this more understandable.

Pain is an unpleasant feeling that in most cases is due to some uncomfortable stimulus. Usually a stimulus that produces pain is one that causes damage to tissue. Thus pain is actually a protective mechanism to make us aware that tissue damage is taking place. In order for a hurtful stimulus to be perceived as pain, pain pathways in the nervous system must be intact and the subject must be conscious. A person who is anesthetized does not feel pain. Anesthesia can be in the form of general anesthesia, which causes the patient to be totally unaware of his environment; or it may be in the form of local anesthesia, in which case nerve impulses are blocked by the local anesthetic so that the anesthetized part has no feeling.

Pain may be felt in a location distant from its cause.

If an uncomfortable stimulus is present and if pain nerve pathways are intact in a conscious person, pain is perceived. However, this simplistic view cannot explain all kinds of pain. There are many examples in which pain may be due to some abnormal function of the nervous system in which there is no abnormality at the site where the pain is felt. One such condition is thalamic syndrome. Thalamic syndrome consists of pain and other abnormal sensations that may involve one-half of the body. It is a result of damage to the thalamus on the side of the brain opposite to where the pain is located. The most common cause of this damage to the thalamus is a stroke. The thalamus is a center in the brain which receives nearly all kinds of sensory information from sense organs throughout the body. When portions of the thalamus are damaged, as can occur in some kinds of strokes, the thalamus may incorrectly interpret sensations (such as touch and pressure) as pain. When this situation is present, severe pain may be present even though no abnormal stimulus occurs in the area where the pain is located.

Another example of pain perceived at a site distant from where the abnormality is located is that of nerve root pain due to a herniated intervertebral disc in the back. Persons with herniated intervertebral discs in the low back area often feel no pain at the site of the abnormality, but rather they experience pain in the distribution of the sciatic nerve down the leg and even in the foot and toes. Patients with amputation of an arm or leg may have phantom limb pain that feels like it is located in the missing extremity. There are other conditions in which pain is felt in part of the body that is distant from the disease process. So pain can be due to malfunction of the brain or other parts of the nervous system and is not necessarily caused by an abnormality in the area where the pain is located.

Pain affected by emotions.

The presence and severity of pain can be greatly influenced by our attention to, or attitude toward, the cause of the pain. Examples can be given of soldiers in battle or persons who are in a fight, who sustain serious injury but do not feel any significant pain as long as their complete attention is given to the activity in which they are engaged. Conversely, pain or headache may be increased by anxiety or fear concerning the seriousness of the cause of these symptoms. A person who believes his headache is due to a brain tumor may have lessening of his symptoms if he learns that no tumor is present.

The above observations being true, it would not be entirely unexpected that in some cases of mental illness, pain or headache could occur when the brain is malfunctioning even though no tumor, infection, or other serious abnormality can be demonstrated. Mental illness does cause headache and pain in some instances, and this pain may be very real to the individual who has this symptom. Feelings of anger and hostility may accentuate pain that would otherwise be tolerable to the place that it becomes unbearable.

What kind of mental illness can cause headache?

Headaches and other pains that are due to mental illness may be due to any one of several causes. These causes include depression, conversion reaction, delusional states, and hypochondriasis.

To the depressed person, environmental stresses and everyday discomforts that present insignificant problems to the emotionally healthy individual may seem to be so great that they are intolerable. Minor pains or headache may become incapacitating to the depressed person. When the

RELIEF FROM HEADACHE

depression is successfully treated, these patients often get remarkable relief from headache and other pains as well.

Conversion reaction consists of an abnormal mental response in which anxiety and stress that become intolerable are "converted" to physical symptoms. One of the most dramatic of conversion reactions is false paralysis. This type of conversion brings a partial solution to the patient's psychological problems in that he is no longer capable of functioning and for this reason can assume a "sick role" and get away from the stress producing situation. Incapacitating headaches may occur by a similar mechanism, but this cause of headache is uncommon. Sometimes it is difficult to determine if a patient's false symptoms — including pain or headache — are due to conversion, which is considered to be on an unconscious level, or malingering, which is on a conscious level.

Delusional symptoms, including delusional headaches, may also result from mental illness. This, too, is uncommon; but when it occurs, it usually happens in a person who has schizophrenia or severe depression. For example, if a person believes that his headaches are caused by a portion of his brain rotting away or due to some abnormal object that has been placed in his head by some other individual to torment him, delusional thinking is present. Abnormal thought patterns and behavior observed in the person who has delusional symptoms, including headache, may help in arriving at the correct diagnosis.

Hypochondriasis is also a form of delusional thinking in which a person has a preoccupation with disease that is not present. In its more persistent and severe forms, it may be a symptom of schizophrenia.

HEADACHE ASSOCIATED WITH MENTAL ILLNESS

All kinds of disease processes may be imitated by mental illness, and all kinds of symptoms of disease may be manifested in patients with this problem. In most instances, however, there are other evidences of mental illness in addition to the symptoms of which the patient complains. Management of these cases can be best accomplished by a psychiatrist who can diagnose the presence of, and the type of, mental illness and then treat the mental illness as well as give treatment for symptomatic management of the headache or other symptoms which are present.

Chronic headache can be a manifestation of a "pain-prone syndrome." Blumer and Heilbronn[1] have attempted to explain some cases of chronic pain, in which no cause for the pain can be identified, as a variant of depression. The depression manifests itself as chronic pain of any one of several kinds, including chronic headache. Persons with this pain-prone syndrome may complain of continuous pain which is of obscure origin and which cannot be explained by the presence of any disease process. These individuals usually have a strong desire for surgery, which they believe will cure their pain. Their preoccupation with pain frequently prevents them from effectively performing normal activity. These people are usually solid citizens who deny any emotional problems and claim to have ideal family relations and work situations. A history of being a "workaholic" is not uncommon. After the pain syndrome begins, there is lack of initiative, inactivity, fatigue, and inability to enjoy social life, sex, or leisure activities. Those affected frequently have difficulty sleeping, which they attribute to the pain. There is usually a mood of despair, and some become alcoholics. Pain or headache becomes a way of life; yet no cause for the pain is found. Many of these patients have unnecessary surgery and are given excessive medication.

According to Blumer and Heilbronn, traditional psychotherapy is not useful for this group of patients. They believe analgesics or antianxiety agents, such as Valium and Librium, are contraindicated because these drugs produce dependence and tend to exacerbate the depression and pain. Treatment with antidepressant drugs, such as Elavil, and behavior modification with gradual rehabilitation back to normal activity and a normal lifestyle are the most effective management. Some individuals who have been diagnosed as having chronic muscle-contraction headache may fit into this group of persons who mask their feelings of guilt and depression with chronic incapacitating headache. The fact that no serious disease is found does not prove that the headache is imaginary. Pain can be due to factors other than serious disease. As Publius Syrus said in the first century B.C., "The pain of the mind is worse than the pain of the body."[1]

Pain and headache may be exaggerated for secondary gain.

When headaches or other painful conditions are due to causes other than disease, injury, or other physical abnormalities — and if they are not due to emotional stress — they are due to malingering more frequently than they are due to genuine mental illness.

In our highly mechanized and well-insured society, persons who are injured often have a strong economic interest in maintaining symptoms and abnormalities due to that injury. Those injured in automobile accidents or in the course of their employment may obtain financial advantages and maintain disability as a means of secondary gain by exaggerating their abnormalities of function and their pain. Secondary gain can be defined as material advantage or emotional satisfaction which may involve financial gain or compensated disability or some other benefit from exaggeration or fabrication of symptoms or abnormalities. Cases of this kind are not infrequent, and they account for much of the litigation regarding personal injury and much of the unnecessarily prolonged disability that occur in our society. Information about the massive amount of unjustified, exaggerated and fraudulent claims of personal injury that are allowed by our legal system is documented in my report **A Study of 249 Patients with Litigated Claims of Injury**[2] and the book **Lawyers, Litigants and Whores**.[3]

Headache can be due to many different causes, and sometimes it actually can be due to mental illness; but this cause of headache is overdiagnosed.

References for Chapter 12.

1. Blumer D, Heilbronn M. Chronic pain as a variant of depressive disease. The pain-prone syndrome. J of Nervous and Mental Disease 1982;170:381-406.
2. Peterson DI. A study of 249 patients with litigated claims of injury. The Neurologist 1998;4:131-137.
3. Peterson DI. Lawyers, Litigants and Whores. St. Louis: Warren H. Green, Inc. (Epoch Press) 2004.

13

Headache Associated with Systemic Disease

Headache can be caused by many diseases.

Headache is a common symptom and it can be associated with any disease. In some instances, however, it may be caused by fever, stress, or other factors occurring in association with the disease process rather than being due directly to the disease itself. In these cases, headache is only indirectly related to the disease with which it is associated. Most diseases that affect any portion of the head can produce headache; but in addition, some systemic diseases which affect parts of the body other than the head also characteristically cause headache. This does not establish that there are as many kinds of headaches as there are kinds of diseases. Regardless of what disease the headache is associated with, it is in all likelihood caused by one of the mechanisms described in chapter 1. The discussion of disease that cause headache presented in this chapter will emphasize mechanisms by which various disease processes produce this symptom. It is not just a list of diseases with which headache can in some way be associated either directly or indirectly.

HEADACHE ASSOCIATED WITH SYSTEMIC DISEASE

Headache often results from inadequate oxygen

Lack of oxygen to the brain can cause headache. At least one result of lack of oxygen is dilation of blood vessels. In this sense the mechanism of production of headache in conditions that decrease oxygen in the brain is similar to that which occurs in classic migraine since both may be associated with dilation of blood vessels. Any condition that interferes with the transfer of oxygen from lungs to the blood — such as pneumonia, emphysema, and congestive heart failure — can cause headache. Obstruction of the respiratory passages, causing asphyxia due to any one of several causes, can have a similar effect. Abnormalities of the blood, such as anemia which decrease the ability of the blood to carry oxygen from the lungs to the brain, can also cause headache. The common denominator of all these conditions is insufficient delivery of oxygen to the brain; and when this occurs, blood vessels dilate by a reflex mechanism. This dilation of blood vessels is an attempt on the part of the body to increase blood flow to the brain and thus increase delivery of oxygen so the brain can function normally; but this reflex blood vessel dilation frequently causes pain in the head. Increase in content of carbon dioxide in the blood may be associated with conditions that cause abnormal function of the lungs. This will also cause dilation of blood vessels resulting in headache.

High blood pressure usually does not cause headache.

It is commonly believed that high blood pressure causes headache. This may be true in cases of severe hypertension, but it is not the case for most persons who have this condition.

RELIEF FROM HEADACHE

Research studies of groups of patients who have hypertension of mild to moderate degree have demonstrated that this is not a common cause of headache. There are many causes for high blood pressure, but at least in some cases, stress of various kinds — including unexpressed anger, anxiety, and frustration, as well as other emotional problems — can be factors in causing increase in blood pressure. The same stress factors that cause high blood pressure may also cause headache; so both of these conditions may in some cases be related to emotional tension rather than headache being secondary to high blood pressure.

Severe hypertension can cause headache. One example of this is the high blood pressure due to adrenal tumors called pheochromocytomas. These tumors of the adrenal gland may intermittently secrete large amounts of norepinephrine, a substance which constricts blood vessels. Surges of increased blood pressure due to intermittent effect of norepinephrine may cause headache. When the surge of high blood pressure occurs, a whole group of symptoms may be present. These include headache, perspiration, tremulousness, pounding of the heart, nausea, and other uncomfortable feelings. The actual cause of headache that occurs with these surges of hypertension has not been established, but it may be due to the stretching effect on the blood vessel walls resulting from the sudden elevation of blood pressure. In this case, dilation of blood vessels does not appear to be the primary cause of headache because blood vessel constriction occurs during these periods. In most cases in which headache is actually due to severely elevated blood pressure the headache is effectively treated when the blood pressure is controlled with antihypertensive medications. In the case of pheochromocytoma, blood pressure is controlled when

HEADACHE ASSOCIATED WITH SYSTEMIC DISEASE

the tumor is surgically removed. In some cases in which the tumor is not diagnosed the blood pressure may go so high that fatal brain hemorrhage occurs. Some kinds of kidney disease that cause hypertension and kidney failure may also cause headache. A few drugs and medicines — including some of the drugs of abuse, such as amphetamine, cocaine and similar substances — can cause elevation of blood pressure. If these drugs are taken in large doses the increase in blood pressure may be severe enough to cause headache. In occasional cases fatal brain hemorrhage occurs from these drugs.

Inflammation or infection often causes headache.

Infections located anywhere in the body, especially if they are accompanied by fever, frequently cause headache by the mechanisms discussed in chapter 7.

Any disease that causes inflammation or destruction of bone may cause pain. If these destructive changes occur in the vertebrae of the neck, headache often results. Some of the diseases that can cause headache by producing abnormalities of the cervical vertebrae include rheumatoid arthritis, bone tumor, bone infections, and any other condition that causes bone destruction. One of the chief means by which headache is produced in these conditions is by painful, sustained spasm of the neck muscles secondary to the pain of the disease process; but headache can also be directly due to bone destruction if it involves the periosteum. Headache may also be due to diseases that affect skull bones. These diseases include tumors, infections, and several well-recognized but uncommon conditions that cause destruction or deformity of bone. These include Paget's disease, multiple myeloma, fibrous dysplasia, and several others.

Headaches caused by abnormalities of the neck.

Headache can also result from neck muscle spasm associated with degenerated or herniated intervertebral discs in the neck. These intervertebral discs are like cushions between the vertebrae; and when they degenerate or herniate they may damage the sensory nerve roots. This often causes pain and associated muscle spasm which in turn causes headache. Peterson and associates have demonstrated that a large number of individuals who have herniated discs in the cervical spine have headache as an associate symptom. This headache is frequently relieved when the herniated disc is successfully treated surgically.[1]

The treatment of headache due to disease of the bones of the neck or skull is best accomplished by treatment of the primary disease process. The degree of success of treatment depends upon what kind of disease is causing the abnormality. If the abnormality is a malignant tumor, radiation therapy may produce rapid and dramatic (but usually only temporary) relief of the pain and headache. In some cases of disease of the bone and intervertebral discs of the neck, immobilization of the head and neck by various mechanical devices such as neck collars, halos and traction equipment may also provide relief. The long-term results, however, depend on whether or not the disease process causing the headache can be successfully treated.

HEADACHE ASSOCIATED WITH SYSTEMIC DISEASE

Temporal arteritis.

A serious disease that occurs chiefly in elderly people which characteristically causes headache as one of its most prominent symptoms is temporal arteritis. This condition causes inflammatory changes in the walls of the arteries. When the arteries of the scalp are involved by this disease severe headache can occur. In most cases of temporal arteritis other blood vessels are also affected, including those inside the head and in other parts of the body. When this process affects the arteries inside the head it can cause strokes. Or if the blood vessels supplying the eye are affected sudden blindness may result. Early diagnosis is important because treatment may prevent these complications. The headache of temporal arteritis is usually very severe and persistent. It is usually located in the temple where there may be tender swellings of the arteries; but the headache and blood vessel abnormalities can occur in any part of the head. Frequently there is pain in the jaws which is aggravated by chewing. In some cases muscle aches and pains occur throughout the body. Associated abnormalities include anemia and an increase in red blood cell sedimentation rate. The diagnosis of temporal arteritis is made on the basis of the symptoms and clinical findings mentioned above, and it is confirmed by cutting out a section of one of the involved arteries for microscopic examination. If the diagnosis is made soon enough, treatment with cortisone-like drugs, such as prednisone, can give good relief of symptoms; and, in many cases, complications such as strokes and blindness due to this condition can be prevented.

RELIEF FROM HEADACHE

Headache can be a side effect of medication.

Since many kinds of medication may lead to headache as a side effect, the medications used for treatment of a disease rather than the disease itself may be the cause of headache. One example is that of nitroglycerin and other drugs used to dilate the coronary arteries of the heart in treatment of angina pectoris. These drugs also dilate blood vessels in other areas, including those in the scalp and in the meninges covering the brain; and they can produce severe headache. The number of medications that can cause headache is too numerous to mention, but fortunately most of these substances produce headache in only a small percentage of persons who use them rather than in everyone who takes them. About half of the drugs listed in *The Physician's Desk Reference* (PDR) list headache as a possible side effect.

Diseases of blood vessels can cause headache.

Several kinds of vascular disease, in addition to those discussed in chapter 6, can cause headaches. Cerebral infarction is the most common kind of stroke, and headache is frequently associated with this condition. Headache may even be present for several hours before the other symptoms of the stroke are noticed. This kind of headache may result from dilation of blood vessels due to lack of oxygen beyond the point of partial or complete occlusion of the blood vessel.

Headache may occur in transient ischemic attacks.

Transient cerebral ischemic attacks are like temporary

HEADACHE ASSOCIATED WITH SYSTEMIC DISEASE

strokes. They may cause transient paralysis or numbness on one side of the body, loss of vision on one side, loss of equilibrium, loss of speech, and several other symptoms. They may result from small blood clots or pieces of cholesterol that have come loose from the blood vessel walls and which are floating in the blood stream. These substances often come from portions of blood vessels that are nearly occluded by arteriosclerosis.

Transient cerebral ischemic attacks may be caused by partial occlusion of one of the carotid arteries of the neck. When this is the case, successful treatment can be accomplished by removing the arteriosclerotic material and blood clots that are causing the blood vessel obstruction. This surgery may prevent a stroke which could occur if the blood vessel becomes completely occluded. However, some individuals also develop severe headache after surgery has been performed to reopen the obstructed blood vessel. The cause of these post-endarterectomy headaches is not known.

Lupus erythematosus is another disease of blood vessels that frequently causes headache. This is a condition in which there are abnormalities of collagen tissue throughout the body. The cause of these headaches is not known, but it is likely that in most cases they are due to blood vessel abnormalities. Abnormalities of fibrous tissue in the neck and neck muscle spasm may also be factors in production of these headaches.

Summary.

The symptom of headache may occur in nearly all diseases and it can be due to a variety of causes. However, the number of headaches due to systemic disease is far less than the number of headaches which are due to painful neck muscle and fibrous tissue contraction which is unrelated to any serious disease process.

References for Chapter 13.

1. Peterson DI, Austin GM, Dayes LA. Headache assocaited with discogenic disease of the cervical spine. Bull Los Angeles Neurol Soc 1975;40:96-100.

14

Headache Caused by Abnormalities of the Eyes, Ears, Nose, Sinuses and Teeth, and the Cranial Neuralgias

Headache caused by eye disease.

Diseases of the eye can be very painful. Pain from eye disease may spread to other parts of the head and in some cases it may be interpreted as headache rather than eye pain. In other cases severe headache is secondary to recognized eye disease, such as infection or glaucoma. Glaucoma consists of increased pressure in the eye which if allowed to continue may cause loss of vision as well as continued severe pain and headache. This is especially true of acute angle closure glaucoma. Glaucoma can occur at any age, but it is uncommon below the age of forty. However, it should be considered in any elderly person who develops eye pain, blurred vision, or redness of the eye associated with headache. Even though pain and headache are often caused by increased pressure in the eye, some cases of chronic glaucoma may cause loss of vision without producing significant pain, headache, or any other discomfort.

Glaucoma is diagnosed by testing the pressure in the eye by any one of several different methods; and this is usually part of an eye examination in patients over forty years of age, even if they have no eye pain. If increased pressure is found, there are several types of medication that can be used to decrease the pressure and thus alleviate symptoms and prevent deterioration of vision. In cases of acute angle closure glaucoma, the kind that is most likely to produce severe pain and headache, eye drops and medication are often not adequate to combat the increased pressure. Emergency surgery may be necessary.

Other diseases of the eye which characteristically cause eye pain and often cause an associated headache include infections and eye injuries. In these cases the cause of the pain and headache is usually obvious, and treatment consists of removal of the cause of the abnormality. Infections of the eye can be due to many different causes, including several kinds of viruses and bacteria. These infections can occur in several parts of the eye. Infections on the surface over the white part of the eye are referred to as conjunctivitis and are in most cases relatively easy to treat because they can be treated by medication applied directly to the eye. This is not true, however, of some kinds of superficial infections of the eye, such as herpes of the cornea. Herpes infection of the cornea can be very difficult to treat even though it is on the surface of the eyeball. Infections of the deeper layers of the eye, including the retina and choroid, may be difficult to diagnose and also difficult to treat.

HEADACHE CAUSED BY ABNORMALITIES

Eye injuries, such as corneal abrasions, even if not serious may cause severe eye pain and headache. Tumors of the eye may also be a cause of eye pain and associated headache. They are often insidious in onset and they may be difficult to diagnose early in their course.

Eye strain is an infrequent cause of headache.

Headache due to "eyestrain" is a controversial subject. It does appear that some individuals get relief of headache when they use properly fitted glasses, but this is the exception rather than the rule. When headache is produced by eyestrain, in at least some cases, it is due to painful contraction of muscles of the scalp and even the neck associated with straining the eye muscles in an attempt to see better. These headaches frequently are of muscle-contraction type and are due to the eyestrain only indirectly. Another indirect cause of headache associated with refractive errors is the fear that many people have that their eyesight will deteriorate if they do not have perfectly fitted glasses. There is no evidence that this is true, but if this belief produces anxiety, it can be a cause of headache. Straining of the eyes because of ill-fitting glasses or because of the need for glasses can frequently cause eye pain and irritation, but headache as a direct result of eyestrain is uncommon.

Ear diseases and headache.

Disease of the ear can cause headache. Several abnormalities of the ear, including several types of infections and some tumors, may produce pain. These painful conditions may then cause headache. Conversely, head pain in other areas such as the throat may be referred to the ear. Nerve endings of the fifth, seventh, ninth, and tenth cranial nerves and the nerves that enter the upper portion of the spinal cord supply sensation to various parts of the ear and the region behind the ear. This extensive sensory nerve supply to the region of the ear probably accounts for the frequency of pain being referred from other regions to the ear and from the ear to other parts of the head. Infections in the ears can spread to the mastoid area and also inside the skull to cause meningitis or brain abscess. These complications of ear infections nearly always cause severe headache. Treatment of pain or headache in each of these conditions consists of treatment of the abnormality that is causing these symptoms as well as providing symptomatic relief.

Headache from abnormalities of the nose and sinuses.

Abnormalities of the nose and sinuses can in some cases produce headache.The most common abnormality in this region that causes this symptom is acute infection of the sinuses. This kind of headache may be located in the frontal region, but it can also be referred to other parts of the head. Headache due to chronic sinusitis is a controversial subject and it is often greatly overdiagnosed. Chronic sinusitis is a very common condition and chronic headache is a very common condition. There is a tendency to believe that the sinusitis is the cause of the headache if they occur

HEADACHE CAUSED BY ABNORMALITIES

together, but in most cases this is not true. Chronic sinusitis rarely causes pain or headache unless there is obstruction of flow of secretion from the sinuses. If this happens, acute sinusitis becomes superimposed on the chronic sinusitis. Most cases of so-called "sinus" headache actually fall into the common migraine/muscle-contraction headache group. They can be more successfully treated by the methods described in chapter 2 than by attempts to treat the chronic sinusitis with various medications, nose drops, or inhalers. This may be fortunate since presently available methods for treatment of chronic sinusitis are not very successful. Treatment of acute sinusitis is best accomplished by establishing drainage from the sinuses and treating the infection with antibiotics.

Headaches may occasionally be due to abnormalities of the nasal septum. Most people have some deviation of the septum, but in some individuals it is severe enough to cause obstruction of the outlet of some of the sinuses. This causes recurrent sinusitis and headache may result. Occasionally abscesses or hematomas in the nasal septum may also cause headache. If one of these types of pathology is present, surgery to remove a portion of the cartilage or other abnormalities that are present may be very effective. However, headache caused by abnormalities of the nasal septum is uncommon; so surgery on the nasal septum will relieve headache in only occasional cases.

Tumors of the sinuses and the back part of the nose and nasopharynx are usually serious conditions and very difficult to treat. These tumors are very uncommon, but when present they nearly always eventually produce severe headache. This headache may be located in any part of the head, but it is usually most severe in the back part of the head where the head and neck join. For this reason, this kind of headache may be difficult to distinguish from common muscle-contraction headache when it first begins. CT or MRI scanning may be needed in some cases to diagnose this condition.

Abnormalities of teeth and jaws occasionally cause headache.

Headache may occasionally be due to abnormalities of the jaws and teeth. These include infections and also malocclusion or abnormalities of alignment of the teeth and jaws. Arthritis of the temporomandibular joint, which is the joint by which the lower jaw attaches to the skull and which allows chewing movements, can also be a cause of headache. This cause of headache is overdiagnosed. A large amount of unnecessary surgery is done and expensive splints are made to treat headache supposedly due to this cause. In cases in which significant abnormality is actually present, there is pain in the temporomandibular joint associated with chewing; and there is usually tenderness to pressure over this joint.

Neuritis and neuralgia.

There are several types of pain, some of which can be very severe, which are due to disease processes directly affecting the sensory nerves of the head. Most of these conditions are uncommon. The best known is called trigeminal neuralgia, or tic douloureux. The pain of trigeminal neu-

HEADACHE CAUSED BY ABNORMALITIES

ralgia is actually very different from headache in the usual sense. Rather, it consists of brief, severe, knife-like jabs of pain which occur in the face or around the eye. These stabs of pain usually last only a few seconds, but they are very severe. For this reason they can be a serious problem, especially if the pain occurs frequently. These pains are due to abnormalities of the fifth cranial nerve. One of the most common of these abnormalities is that of pressure on the nerve from an abnormal blood vessel which crosses the nerve as it enters the brain stem inside the skull.

Several other types of abnormalities, including tumors and even multiple sclerosis, can also cause trigeminal neuralgia. The most effective medical treatment for this condition is the use of some of the same drugs that are used in the treatment of epilepsy. These drugs are not pain-killing drugs in the usual sense. The names of these drugs are Dilantin and Tegretol. More than 50 percent of cases of trigeminal neuralgia can be controlled by the use of these medications to the extent that pain is no longer a major problem.

If medical treatment is unsatisfactory, there are several surgical procedures which usually decrease or eliminate the pain. A simple commonly used procedure is that of destruction of a portion of the fifth nerve by the use of high frequency electric current. An older type of treatment which is much less effective is that of injection of alcohol into the nerve. This method is often unsatisfactory because relief is of such short duration. Another successful method of treatment for trigeminal neuralgia has been the placement of a small teflon sponge between the fifth nerve and the abnormal blood vessel that is compressing the nerve.

RELIEF FROM HEADACHE

The chief disadvantage of this procedure is that it is a form of brain surgery, and this involves some risk to the patients. However, the pain of trigeminal neuralgia is frequently so severe that in many cases the patient is willing to take that risk if he cannot get relief by more simple methods of treatment. A newer and often very successful treatment for this condition is radiation therapy with the "gamma knife." A similar type of neuralgia may occur in other nerves and may produce similar symptoms in other locations, but since these conditions are very uncommon they will not be described.

Postherpetic neuralgia.

Postherpetic neuralgia is another condition that produces severe head pain, but this too is usually quite different in character from headache. Postherpetic neuralgia is a persistent pain which remains after an attack of shingles or herpes zoster. The organism that causes shingles is the same virus that causes chickenpox. It may remain in a dormant state in the fifth nerve for many years, only to be activated by some type of trauma, surgical procedure, or serious disease. This results in an attack of shingles involving the face and scalp if the fifth nerve is involved. Shingles may also affect the chest or other parts of the body if other nerves are affected. The acute attack of herpes zoster usually lasts only a few weeks and consists of painful blisters of the skin; but after the blisters heal many patients have a continuous chronic burning pain in the area where the blisters were located during the acute attack of shingles. This chronic pain is called postherpetic neuralgia and may persist for many years. In some cases it never resolves. Treatment of herpes zoster in its acute state when the blisters are still present may include the use of cortisone-like drugs and antiviral drugs. This treatment may also decrease the severity of postherpetic neuralgia; but after postherpetic neuralgia develops there is no completely satisfactory treatment. There is, however, a very simple treatment which can be helpful in many cases. It appears to be just as effective as other more complicated treatments such as injections, nerve blocks, and even surgical removal of the painful area. This simple treatment consists of introducing frequent stimuli to the involved area by rubbing it briskly with a damp washcloth. If this type of massage is performed for a period of five to ten minutes every hour or two throughout the day, significant improvement usually occurs in a period of three to four weeks. This treatment may not be effective in all cases; and various medications, nerve blocks, and surgical procedures may be necessary. Unfortunately these types of treatment usually are not very effective either.

Occipital neuralgia.

Occipital neuralgia consists of pain and frequently other sensory symptoms, including numbness and tingling in the back of the head in the distribution of the second cervical nerve. This nerve enters the upper portion of the spinal cord between the first and second cervical vertebrae. The most common form of occipital neuralgia is due to involvement of the greater occipital nerve and is referred to as greater occipital nerve neuralgia. It is due to rather poorly defined pathology of this nerve and can result from several different conditions. In some cases it is caused by arthritic changes in the vertebrae and degenerative changes in the intervertebral discs, resulting in compression or irritation of the nerve roots. More commonly it results from persistent, painful contraction of neck muscles and fibrous tissue, which occur with muscle-contraction or myofascial headache. This causes irritation and compression of the nerve.

Headache from this condition is usually located in the back of the head and is associated with pain in the neck muscle. It may be located on only one side or both sides; but frequently there is referred pain to other parts of the head, even to the forehead and around the eye. This cause of pain and headache is well recognized by most authorities on the subject of headache. Wolff states that "...noxious stimulation of structures supplied by the upper cervical nerves is often followed by spread (of pain) to the forehead and face."[1] This can be easily demonstrated in many patients with greater occipital nerve neuralgia who also have frontal headache. The greater occipital nerve can be blocked with a local anesthetic causing elimination of pain in the distribution of this nerve. Complete but temporary relief of the pain and headache in the frontal and temporal regions and around the eye often follows this procedure. Conversely, eye pain and frontal headache can be experimentally produced by injecting an irritating solution into the muscles of the base of the skull and the upper part of the neck.[2] Although some authorities consider greater occipital nerve neuralgia a rare condition, it is commonly associated with prolonged muscle-contraction headache and abnormalities of the cervical spine such as

HEADACHE CAUSED BY ABNORMALITIES

arthritis and herniated or degenerated intervertebral discs.

Treatment of greater occipital nerve neuralgia by nerve block provides only transient relief. This is not adequate final treatment for headache but it is effective symptomatic treatment and may decrease the need for narcotics when severe attacks of headache occur. More importantly it is a good test to help diagnose the cause of headache. Most persons who get relief from nerve block of the occipital nerves can get rid of their headache by achieving normal mobility of neck muscles and fibrous tissues as described in chapter 2. One would suspect that destroying the greater occipital nerve would produce complete lasting relief. This procedure is done by some neurosurgeons, but relief is usually not permanent unless the cause of pain is also removed. As sensation slowly returns to the area previously supplied by the destroyed nerve, pain and headache also return; and they are then more difficult to treat. Surgical treatment of greater occipital nerve neuralgia is usually neither appropriate nor necessary. Relief can be obtained in most cases within a period of a few weeks by the simple stretching exercise program used for muscle-contraction headaches when normal range of motion is achieved. If there is a tumor or localized infection involving the cervical spine, the neck, or the greater occipital nerve, the appropriate treatment is that which is directed toward specific treatment of the abnormality that is causing the pain.

Several other types of neuralgia may produce headache or head pain, but they are quite rare; so they will not be discussed.

RELIEF FROM HEADACHE

References for Chapter 14.

1. Dalessio DJ. Wolff's headache and other head pains. 3rd ed. New York: Oxford University Press 1972:549.
2. Cyriax J. Rheumatic headache. Brit Med J 1938;2:1367.

15

Other Kinds of Headache

Several types of environmental situations, various kinds of food, and some kinds of activity are associated with headache frequently enough so that the headache is named for that activity or situation. These headaches may be due to several types of pain-producing mechanisms, but they probably all in one way or another fit into the mechanisms of headache production discussed in chapter 1.

Altitude headache.

Headache occurs at high altitudes, and it is one of the symptoms of mountain sickness. The frequency and severity of headache appears to be directly related to the altitude, especially in mountain climbing. If a person becomes gradually acclimatized to high altitudes, headache and mountain sickness are less likely to occur; and if they do occur, they are less severe than in those who are abruptly exposed to high altitudes without an opportunity to become acclimatized. The cause of this headache is not known; but it may be related to several factors, including abnormal blood vessel dilation. Altitude, of itself, does not appear to be the only cause of the headache. Mountain climbers are much more likely to get symptoms at high altitudes than those who fly up to similar altitudes in an airplane. Fatigue may be a significant factor. Lack of oxygen in the air in high altitudes can cause abnormal symptoms and can even cause swelling of the brain from accumulation of fluid, but mountain sickness develops even when an adequate oxygen supply is available. Some veteran mountain climbers report that if they drink a large amount of fluid before and during their mountain climbing activities they are less likely to develop altitude headaches.

Change of weather headache.

Many persons with migraine report that they are more likely to have an attack of migraine when there is a change in the weather. This change is not necessarily of a certain type because some individuals get a headache when it gets colder; some when it gets hotter; some during thunderstorms; and some when the weather is hot, dry, or windy. Some individuals develop headache as well as several other uncomfortable symptoms 12 to 24 hours before the change in weather actually occurs. These other symptoms include irritability, sleeplessness, difficulty in breathing, depression, and other unpleasant feelings. It seems that these symptoms are most likely to occur prior to hot dry windstorms such as the Harmattan of the southern Sahara, the Mistral of France, the Sirocco of the Mediterranean, the Zonda of Argentina, and similar climatic conditions which occur in other parts of the world but which are known by other names characteristic of that region. There have been several attempts to explain these headaches and other symptoms related to changes in the weather. These attempted explanations have included a relationship of the symptoms to the total number of positive or negative ions in the air and changes in humidity causing changes in mood which may then make headaches more likely to occur, but no satisfactory explanation has yet been found. One research study done by Gomersall and Stuart has shown that weather changes relate more to changes in severity of the headache than to frequency of headache.[1] It is likely that many of these headaches are of a muscle-contraction type, but migraine attacks may also occur during changes in the weather.

Sex headache.

Some individuals have headache either during or after sexual intercourse. These headaches can be due directly to the sexual activity and are quite distinct from those of individuals who complain, "Not tonight, Dear, I have a headache," to avoid this relationship (Figure 1). There have been some cases of intracranial hemorrhage due to either a ruptured aneurysm or a vascular malformation and also some cases of hemorrhage from high blood pressure which have occurred during sexual intercourse. It is true that if this occurs these hemorrhages may cause a very severe headache. The cooperative study on vascular disease reported that around four percent of intracranial hemorrhages occur at the time of or somewhere around the time of sexual intercourse.[2] Considering, however, the frequency of intracranial hemorrhage and also the frequency of sexual intercourse, it

RELIEF FROM HEADACHE

Used with the kind permission of Carnick Laboratories, Inc

Figure 1. Headache can threaten marriages as well as interfere with work and social activities.

would not be unusual if these events would occur at about the same time in many cases. This would not necessarily prove that there was a direct cause and effect relationship between them. The same can be said for migraine and muscle-contraction headaches which may also occur during or after sexual intercourse.

On some occasions patients are brought to an emergency room or to a doctor's office because of excruciating headache which develops in relationship to sexual activ-

OTHER KINDS OF HEADACHE

ity. In the author's experience, many of these patients, especially when they are males, have a sexual-emotional problem which usually consists of decreased sexual potency or fatigue after prolonged sexual activity. In most cases no hemorrhage or intracranial disease is found. In some of these cases there has been an inability to perform up to the expectations of the sex partner. There are, however, occasional cases in which individuals experience severe headache related to sexual activity in which none of the above factors appear to be present and for which the cause cannot be identified. Some of these headaches may be of a muscle-contraction type.

Exertional headache.

Exertion produces headache in some individuals. The exertion does not necessarily have to be prolonged. Heavy lifting, sudden straining, or even coughing and retching associated with vomiting may produce head pain that can be severe. Individuals with this kind of headache need to have a neurological examination because brain tumors and other neurological diseases may manifest themselves in this manner. This is especially true if the headache occurs as a sudden pain that is synchronous with exertion or straining. Headache may also be the result of straining muscles when the head and neck are in an uncomfortable or unusual position, especially if this activity is prolonged. In addition, it is not uncommon for individuals who perform any type of work on a hot day to get a headache if they are not used to that kind of activity. This can occur while playing tennis, gardening, or doing anything that requires an unusual amount of muscular effort. Some of these headaches appear to be due to fluid loss from sweating and not drinking adequate amounts of water. Drinking more fluids can prevent some of these headaches. There are reports of some exertional headaches being associated with abscessed teeth, and in these cases if the affected teeth are removed the exertional headaches may be eliminated. Most exertional headaches are not due to serious disease. Many of them can be successfully treated by the methods described in chapter 2. In some cases Indocin, a nonsteroidal antiinflammatory drug, gives relief.

Hangover headache.

That headache is a common symptom of "hangover" is an observation that has been made by many of those who have used alcohol, especially when it has been used to excess. Although the relationship of headache to the use of alcohol is well recognized, the actual cause of hangover headache is not known. Since some believe that there is less hangover headache after drinking vodka than after drinking other types of alcoholic beverages, it has been suggested that impurities in some alcoholic beverages, which also may give them their distinctive flavor, may be the cause of the headaches. This view is somewhat difficult to correlate with the fact that it appears that nearly all of these substances as well as the alcohol itself have been largely metabolized or eliminated from the body when the hangover headache occurs.

Other explanations have been considered. These include electrolyte imbalance and dehydration, both of which can occur from drinking alcohol — especially if it is used in large amounts. Alcohol itself causes dilation of blood vessels, and this may account for the precipitation of migraine and cluster headache by this substance. But this does not appear to explain hangover headaches since the blood alcohol level is usually low when hangover headache is present. The cause of other symptoms that occur along with hangover headaches — such as tremor, nausea, fatigue, faintness, pallor, nervousness, and anxiety — are not very well explained either. It is possible that all of these symptoms are due to withdrawal from the effects of alcohol and a return to normal activity of body functions that have been depressed by the direct effect of alcohol when significant blood levels of this substance were present.

Ice cream headache.

Ice cream headache consists of a rather severe pain, usually located in the forehead but which can be present in nearly all parts of the head, which occurs when cold foods or liquids come in contact with the roof of the mouth and the throat. This pain is usually first experienced in childhood. This may be partially due to the fact that children are more likely than adults to eat ice cream rapidly. It has been reported that persons who have migraine are more likely to experience this type of headache than those who do not have this condition. This pain may be due to constriction of blood vessels to the extent that some of the tissues exposed to the cold substance do not get enough blood supply.

Almost any portion of the body that is placed in ice water will have an aching pain. The mechanism of pain produced in ice cream headache may be similar to that which occurs when a hand or foot or any other part of the body is immersed in ice water for a period of time. This type of pain and ice cream headache are usually of short duration, and they disappear shortly after the cold stimulus is removed. Reflex vasospasm and the direct effect of the cold stimulus may be important factors in causing headaches of this kind.

Headaches produced by food.

Several kinds of food are capable of producing headache in some persons, but this is uncommon. A few individuals who have migraine may be sensitive to certain specific types of food, such as chocolate, fish, strong cheese, certain alcoholic beverages, and even citrus fruit; but the majority of people who have migraine as well as other kinds of headache observe no relationship of their headaches to any specific type of food. Other kinds of food — such as hot dogs, bologna, and several types of lunch meat — contain nitrites and nitrates as food preservatives. These substances can produce headache in nearly everyone if they are used in large quantities. This kind of headache results from dilation of blood vessels by the direct effect of these chemical compounds. It is because of the toxic effect of these substances that the quantity of nitrites and nitrates that can be used in cured meats and other food is limited by government regulations.

Some people who eat Chinese food complain of uncomfortable symptoms, including headache, dizziness, nausea, diarrhea, and abdominal pain. These symptoms are referred

OTHER KINDS OF HEADACHE

to as Chinese restaurant syndrome. They are caused by ingestion of monosodium glutamate, a substance used in soy sauce and, therefore, in most Chinese food. It has been demonstrated that some persons who develop Chinese restaurant syndrome have a deficiency of pyridoxine (vitamin B_6). It has also been shown that the symptoms of Chinese restaurant syndrome can be prevented in some individuals if they take a supplement of vitamin B_6 in a dosage of 50 mg each day for a period of several weeks before ingesting monosodium glutamate.[3]

There may be other instances in which abnormalities of metabolism or certain deficiencies are responsible for headache as well as other symptoms that occur in occasional individuals who seem to be sensitive to certain types of food as well as some kinds of medication. It is a common observation that some kinds of drugs may produce headache in occasional individuals even though the great majority of persons who use them do not experience this problem. Headaches caused by certain foods are more likely to be due to direct effects of substances in those foods than to food allergy. In either case a trial of an elimination diet may be helpful. To accomplish this a person may eliminate one type of food such as wheat or milk from the diet for a period of a few weeks. It is reasonable to begin with the substances mentioned above which are known to cause headache in some people.

Postlumbar punture headache

Many people who have had a lumbar puncture have had a severe headache after this procedure. A lumbar puncture is accomplished by introducing a needle between the spinous processes of the vertebrae in the lower part of the back to obtain spinal fluid. A headache is even more likely to occur after a myelogram. A myelogram differs from a lumbar puncture in that a liquid substance that is opaque to x-rays is introduced into the spinal fluid so that abnormalities of the spinal cord or other abnormalities that occur in the subarachnoid space around the spinal cord can be seen by x-ray. This technique is analogous to using barium in a GI study to identify abnormalities of the stomach and intestines. Most abnormalities of the spinal cord and abnormalities in the subarachnoid space cannot be seen by simple x-ray techniques. Therefore in order to identify a tumor, herniated disc, or other disease process, the x-ray-opaque substance is injected into the subarachnoid space so structural abnormalities in this space can be visualized. Myelography is done much less frequently since CT and MRI are available.

Another test that is done by introducing a needle into the spinal canal is a pneumoencephalogram. When a pneumoencephalogram is done, air is injected into the subarachnoid space so that it flows around the spinal cord and into the head. Air is much less dense to x-ray than are brain tissue and spinal fluid so when air enters the ventricles these structures can be seen on x-rays taken while the air is present. Hydrocephalus (enlargement of the ventricles), tumors, and other abnormalities inside the head can be seen by this means. This procedure nearly always produces a severe headache. The headache is thought to be due to the irritation caused by the air contracting pain-sensitive structures. As long as the air is inside the ventricles, pain is not very severe, but when it overflows from the ventricles over the surface of

OTHER KINDS OF HEADACHE

the brain, severe headache results. This test is done rarely now because CT and MRI can give most of the information that can be obtained by pneumoencephalography. Before CT and MRI were available many pneumoencephalograms were done to assist in diagnosis of brain disease.

Headaches that occur after lumbar puncture can be very severe when the patient is sitting or standing, but they usually disappear rapidly if the patient lies down with his head lower than the body or at the same level as the body. The cause of this headache is ongoing leakage of spinal fluid into the soft tissues of the back outside the subarachnoid space after the needle has been withdrawn. Normally the spinal fluid helps support the brain much as if it were floating in a container of water. When insufficient spinal fluid is present, and when the person is in an upright position, the brain actually sags downward — causing stretching of pain-sensitive structures. It has been demonstrated that post spinal puncture headache can be relieved by injecting fluid into the subarachnoid space to replace that fluid which has leaked out. Post spinal puncture headache usually lasts only a short period of time because the hole in the arachnoid membrane that allows leakage of spinal fluid closes to allow a normal amount of spinal fluid to accumulate. In a few cases, post spinal puncture headache has lasted for several weeks or even as long as a month or two. If prolonged headache occurs it can be terminated by injecting some of the patient's own blood drawn from a vein into the region where the leakage of spinal fluid occurs. This causes closure of the leak so that a normal amount of spinal fluid can accumulate, and this stops the headache. This procedure is referred to as a "blood patch" because of its effect of patching the hole where the spinal fluid is leaking out. It has been observed that the larger the needle used in doing a lumbar puncture and the longer it is left in place, the more likely the patient is to develop a post spinal puncture headache. Occasionally, in back injuries, the arachnoid membrane is torn. This can produce the same kind of headache that occurs after lumbar puncture even though no lumbar puncture has been done.

Dialysis headache.

Another medical procedure that very commonly causes headache is dialysis. This procedure is used to treat patients with kidney failure who are no longer able to urinate or pass adequate urine to get rid of waste products in the body. Although patients with kidney failure often develop severe headaches from accumulation of these waste products, the headache may be even more severe after they have had dialysis — especially if the dialysis removes a large amount of this waste material rapidly. Dialysis headache often disappears or is at least less severe after the damaged kidneys have been surgically removed. This suggests that the headache may in some way be related to impaired function of the diseased kidneys, which results in abnormal fluid and electrolyte balance, changes in blood pressure, and changes in the level of some hormones that are related to kidney function and blood pressure.

Withdrawal headache.

Withdrawal of a drug to which a person has become addicted, or upon which he has become dependent, frequently causes headaches. This may occur after addiction to hard drugs such as morphine or heroin, and it commonly occurs in alcohol withdrawal. Severe headache may also occur after withdrawal from ergot when the use of ergot compounds for the treatment of migraine has been abused. But the most common kind of withdrawal headache occurs on withdrawal from caffeine. Many heavy coffee drinkers have morning headaches which are actually due to the withdrawal from caffeine that takes place during the sleeping hours. These headaches are usually promptly relieved by drinking a cup of coffee. Most individuals who discontinue the use of coffee or tea, and especially if they have been using large amounts of these beverages, experience headaches which can be very severe for a period of three to four days. In any type of withdrawal, the symptoms are less severe if the individual withdraws gradually from the substance he has been abusing rather than "cold turkey." The mechanism of headache production on withdrawal from various drugs and beverages is not known. In most cases it probably results from dilation of blood vessels that occurs due to removal of the effect of substances which normally cause the blood vessels to constrict. Overactivity of other normal bodily functions that have been suppressed by the drug that has been abused may also be a factor.

Postseizure headache.

Headache frequently occurs after an epileptic seizure, especially if it is of the generalized tonic-clonic or grand mal type. This kind of headache may be due to several causes including blood vessel dilation and muscle contraction

RELIEF FROM HEADACHE

related to the seizure.

Other causes of headache.

There are many other special situations and environment-related factors that could be mentioned which can cause headache. The headache is often named for the situation or environmental factor to which the headache is thought to be related. A whole list of such headaches is given on page 14. It is likely that most of these headaches are of the muscle-contraction type; but in some cases they may consist of migraine, which occurs in special situations in headache susceptible individuals. Many of these headaches can be managed successfully by following the simple instructions outlined in chapter 2.

Summary.

Headache, man's most common pain, has caused great suffering throughout history and has seriously interfered with the activity and lifestyle of many people. Although it may be a first warning of the presence of serious disease, this is uncommon. Usually it is just a curse and affliction that brings suffering to mankind. Although it is unlikely that headaches will ever be completely eradicated, most people with this problem can gain a better understanding of headache and its causes and also obtain relief from most common kinds of headaches by utilizing the information in this book.

References for Chapter 15.

1. Gomersall JD, Stuart A. Variations in migraine attacks with changes in weather conditions. Int J Biometeorol 1973;17:285-299.
2. Locksley HB. Natural history of subarachnoid hemorrhage. J Neurosurg 1966;25:219-240.
3. Folkers K, Shizukuishi S, Scudder SL, et al. Biochemical evidence for a deficiency of vitamin B_6 in subjects reacting to monosodium L-glutamate by the Chinese restaurant syndrome. Biochemical and Biophysical Res Commun 1981;100:972-977.

16

Effects and Side Effects of Drugs Used to Treat Headache

More than one hundred kinds and combinations of drugs have been used for treatment of headache. Many of these substances can be obtained over-the-counter without a prescription. There are many different names for these over-the-counter headache remedies, but most of them contain aspirin, acetaminophen, caffeine, ibuprofen, antihistamines and vasoconstrictors in various combinations. Long continued use has shown that most of these drugs are relatively safe but even they occasionally produce serious side effects. Prescription medications for headache include an even larger variety of drugs. They too are relatively safe if used according to directions. These medications produce symptomatic relief which can be very helpful for acute headaches but when used over a long period of time some of them cause drug dependence and serious complications. The greatest shortcoming of these headache medications is that in most cases they do not combat the cause of headache but rather they provide only symptomatic relief.

It would be nearly impossible to describe every drug that has been used for treatment of headache, but in the following pages most of the kinds of drugs that are recognized as being effective for this purpose will be discussed.

Ergot alkaloids.

Alkaloids, all of which come from plants, are organic compounds containing carbon, nitrogen, oxygen, and hydrogen. Ergot alkaloids were first found in fungus that grows on rye plants. Some of the toxic effects of these drugs were known long before their therapeutic uses were discovered. The history of some of the tragic results of taking these substances unknowingly is mentioned in chapter 9. Newer and safer drugs have largely replaced ergot preparations for treatment of headache.

Ergot was first used in the treatment of headache in the form of ergotamine tartrate in the latter part of the nineteenth century. Traditionally its beneficial effect in treatment of headache has been attributed to its ability to constrict blood vessels. This constriction of blood vessels was thought to counteract the dilation of blood vessels occurring in migraine. There are, however, some inconsistencies in this theory. (1) Ergot is beneficial for headaches that are unrelated to abnormalities of blood vessels. Horton,[1] Barrie,[2] and others found that ergot helps muscle-contraction headaches as well as migraine so its benefit is not confined to relief of headaches that are associated with abnormal dilation of blood vessels. (2) Some of the ergot preparations that relieve headache have no significant vasoconstrictor effect but rather they may even produce dilation of blood vessels. These are the ergot compounds that are saturated with hydrogen such as dihydroergotamine. This drug blocks sympathetic nervous system activity and thus constriction of blood vessels is counteracted.

The effects of these drugs on blood vessels may not be the means by which they produce a beneficial effect against headache. Their action may be on the brain itself to block neurotransmitters and by this means decrease pain, or these drugs may prevent or decrease headache by some as yet undiscovered mechanism.

Ergot preparations produce their best therapeutic effect if they are given for migraine before the headache begins but after the warning of the headache has started. They can also be used on a regular daily basis to prevent headaches. Used in this manner ergot has a significant drug dependency producing potential.

There are several different preparations of ergot and this substance can be given by several routes. It can be given orally, intramuscularly, or intravenously, and in addition it can be inhaled. It can be absorbed through the rectal mucosa when used in the form of suppositories. It can also be placed under the tongue to be absorbed across the mucous membrane of the mouth. The most commonly used ergot preparations and the routes by which they are administrated are shown in Table 1. This table, as well as all the other tables in this chapter, lists drugs representative of the drug group, but not necessarily all the drugs in each group. Representative dosage forms are also given.

The toxicity of ergot has been mentioned in chapter

EFFECTS AND SIDE EFFECTS OF DRUGS

Table 1

Ergot Drugs

Generic	Brand Name*	Method of Administration
Ergotamine**	Ergomar	Sublingual tablets 2.0 mg
	Ergostat	Sublingual tablets 2.0 mg
	Medihaler-Ergotamine	By inhalation
Methylergonovine***	Methergine	Tablets 0.2 mg. Or by injection
Dihydroergotamine	D.H.E.-45	By injection
Methysergide	Sansert	Tablets 2.0 mg

* Trade name by which the drug is marketed.

** There are several combinations of ergotamine with other compounds. These include Cafergot, Wigraine, and Bellergal.

*** This drug is used in obstetrics. It has not yet been approved by the Food and Drug Administration (FDA) for headache.

9. Gangrene is the most serious. This complication will probably not occur if the drug is used according to directions. Nevertheless, it has been established that persons with disease of the blood vessels such as hardening of the arteries are more susceptible to damage from ergot drugs. They may experience obstruction of these vessels when vasoconstriction takes place. Patients with infection or liver disease are more likely to get complications than those who do not have these pre-existing problems. It is possible that even the usual therapeutic dose of these drugs could cause complications in

these persons.

Some patients cannot tolerate ergot because it causes nausea and vomiting. This is especially undesirable in patients who have migraine because nausea and vomiting also occur with this kind of headache and they can be made worse by ergot medication. There is some danger of heart attack in elderly individuals who have coronary artery disease. The ergot drugs also cause contraction of uterine muscle so they may cause abortion in persons who are pregnant. This ability to contract uterine muscle is used beneficially after delivery of babies to cause the uterus to contract and thus decrease blood loss. Numbness and tingling of the extremities may be caused by ergot. This may be due to constriction of the blood vessels causing impairment of circulation. Muscle weakness may also occur. In higher dosages than are recommended for therapeutic use, ergot drugs can cause confusion, unconsciousness, and epileptic type seizures. In spite of all these side effects and dangers, ergot drugs can be used safely in most people if recommended doses are not exceeded.

Methysergide (Sansert) is a synthetic ergot-like drug that is effective in prevention of migraine and cluster headache. It is closely related chemically to LSD. It is a serotonin blocking agent. It is for this reason that it was first used to prevent headache because it has long been suspected that abnormalities of function of the neurotransmitter serotonin may be involved in the cause of migraine. Methysergide is effective in the prevention of either migraine or cluster headache, but it has not been used effectively for the acute treatment of either one of these conditions. This drug has weak ability to constrict blood vessels as compared to some of the naturally occurring ergot alkaloids. For this reason it

EFFECTS AND SIDE EFFECTS OF DRUGS

is less likely to cause acute obstruction of blood vessels. But it has another dangerous side effect that limits its use. It may produce an inflammatory fibrosis around the blood vessels that supply the kidneys, lungs, and other organs if it is used over a longer period of time. For this reason it is safest not to use this drug for a period longer than 4 to 6 months without a drug holiday. The fibrosis around the blood vessels which can cause failure of function of the organs supplied by these vessels usually regresses when the drug is withdrawn. If this condition is not recognized and the drug is continued, severe damage to the kidneys and other organs may occur. There are several other less commonly known ergot drugs and synthetic preparations of ergot that are used for other purposes; for example, bromocriptine is used in treatment of abnormalities of the pituitary gland and for Parkinson's disease. These other ergot drugs have not as yet been used for treatment of headache. Ergot drugs are available by prescription only.

Aspirin and other nonsteroidal antiinflammatory drugs.

Aspirin, also known as acetylsalicylic acid, is a synthetic salicylate first used as a therapeutic agent in the nineteenth century. Naturally occurring salicylates come from plant sources such as willow bark and some kinds of fruit trees. Medicinal preparations from these sources are said to have been used by Hippocrates nearly 2,400 years ago.[3] It is unclear, however, whether these preparations were used for headache. It is believed that they were used for treatment of infections and several other medical conditions but it is possible that they were also used for treatment of headache over

RELIEF FROM HEADACHE

2,000 years ago. There are references from the literature of the middle ages about use of bark containing salicylates for medicinal purposes.

In the last 30 years several aspirin-like compounds have been synthesized. These drugs are classified as non-narcotic analgesics because they do not cause addiction or drowsiness. The most common use for these substances is in treatment of arthritis but several of them have been used for

Table 2

Aspirin and Other Nonsteroidal Antiinflammatory Drugs

Generic	Brand Name	Method of Administration
Acetylsalicylic acid*	Aspirin**	Tablets 325 mg
Diflunisal	Dolobid	Tablets 250, 500 mg
Indomethacin	Indocin**	Tablets 25, 50 mg. Or by injection
Sulindac	Clinoril	Tablets 100, 200 mg
Phenylbutazone	Butazolidin	Tablets 100 mg
Naproxen*	Anaprox, Naprosyn**	Tablets 250, 500 mg
Meclofenamate	Meclomen	Tablets 50, 100 mg
Mefenamic acid	Ponstel	Tablets 250 mg
Ibuprofen*	Motrin, Advil, & others**	Tablets 200, 600, 800 mg
Fenoprofen	Nalfon**	Tablets 200 mg. Or by injection
Ketoprofen	Orudis**	Tablets 25, 50 mg
Piroxicam	Feldene	Capsules 10, 20 mg
Tolmetin	Tolectin	Capsules 200 mg
Diclofenac	Voltaren	Tablets 25, 50 mg

* Available over-the-counter without a prescrption as individual drugs and in combination with other drugs.

** Controlled studies have found these drugs effective against headache. Not all these drugs are FDA approved for this purpose. All the drugs in Table 3 are FDA approved for treatment of pain.

EFFECTS AND SIDE EFFECTS OF DRUGS

treatment of headache. The ones that are most widely used to treat headache are ibuprofen and naproxen, but it is likely that all of these substances can give some symptomatic relief from headache (Table 2). These drugs act by inhibiting the effects of inflammation and they counteract fever. They also decrease sensitivity to pain. They decrease the formation and release of prostaglandins from normal body cells. Prostaglandins can cause headache if they are experimentally injected into a person who is not susceptible to headache. The headaches they produce in this situation are like severe migraine but it is not known for certain that inhibition of prostaglandins is the mechanism by which aspirin and similar drugs prevent headache.

Aspirin and its more recently synthesized drug family members produce irritation of the lining of the stomach which may cause peptic ulcer and gastrointestinal hemorrhage which can be very severe. There is a great individual variability in susceptibility to this side effect in that some people can take large doses of these drugs and have no recognized damage to the lining of the stomach, whereas others may hemorrhage from low doses of these medications. Liver damage may occasionally occur from some of these drugs. This is uncommon if they are not used excessively. Aspirin has an effect on the blood which makes hemorrhage more likely from any source and in some persons it produces easy bruisability. This is due at least in part to its antiplatelet effect. It is by this mechanism that a low dose of aspirin each day may decrease the likelihood of strokes and heart attacks.

Some of these drugs also produce anemia and other abnormalities of the blood. Occasional fatal reactions have occurred from these substances due to an unpredictable allergic response which causes airway obstruction and inability to breathe. Even aspirin has occasionally done this. Some of these medications have also produced kidney failure. As in the case with most other medications these drugs are usually safe if not taken in overdose. However, if any unusual symptoms occur from these drugs their use should be discontinued. Several of the aspirin-like drugs have been withdrawn from the market because of the high incidence of toxic and allergic reactions they have caused.

Indomethacin, which is one of the aspirin-like drugs, has been found to be very effective for some kinds of headache that respond poorly to other medications. These include a variant of cluster headaches called chronic paroxysmal hemicrania. This headache syndrome consists of multiple brief attacks of severe headache each day with complete clearing of symptoms between each attack. It is a very rare condition. Indomethacin has also been reported to be effective in some headaches related to exertion, coughing, or straining. Classic migraine may also be benefited by this drug. Paradoxically this drug may cause headache in as many as 30 to 40 percent of people who use it for arthritis or some other purpose.

Ibuprofen, which is another aspirin-like drug, is effective against headache. It is marketed over-the-counter as Advil, Rufen, Nuprin, and by several other names. Naproxin is available over-the-counter as Aleve.

Other non-narcotic analgesics.

Phenacetin is a synthetic analgesic derived from coal tar which was very popular as a treatment for headache as well as for arthritis pain and it was widely used before it was

EFFECTS AND SIDE EFFECTS OF DRUGS

found to produce kidney failure. This drug was often used in combination with aspirin and caffeine as Empirin, APC, and other proprietary over-the-counter medications. Phenacetin has not been marketed in this country for several years because of its association with kidney failure. It is believed that in the past it was responsible for kidney failure in about 10 percent of patients who required dialysis or kidney transplantation.

    Acetaminophen, which is the chief metabolite of phenacetin, is marketed in the United States as Tylenol and by several other trade names. Acetaminophen accounts for about one-third of over-the-counter analgesic market in the United States. It has been considered one of the safest medications for headache and other kinds of pain because it does not have the tendency to produce ulceration of the stomach and bleeding from the stomach as aspirin does. It appears, however, that it has a slight potential to produce kidney failure as does its parent substance phenacetin. Some studies show that persons who take acetaminophen frequently may have three times the likelihood of developing kidney failure as those who take aspirin or who use acetaminophen only occasionally.[4] Although these commonly used over-the-counter medications that are used to treat pain and headache are safe for most people it is well known that some people are hypersensitive to them and may get severe adverse responses. It is also well known that abuse of these medications by excessive daily use can produce life threatening complications. Acetaminophen taken in large doses, especially in persons such as alcoholics who may have some impairment of liver function, can cause fatal liver failure.[5]

RELIEF FROM HEADACHE

Narcotic analgesics.

Opium, which contains several narcotic alkaloids including morphine and codeine, has been used for centuries to treat pain. Opium was used by the Greeks before the time of Christ. Since then it has been widely used throughout most of the world for treatment of pain. Its potential for causing addiction has been known for many years. It was available in this country as an over-the-counter medication until 1914 when the Harrison Narcotic Act was passed. There are many similar preparations. There are several synthetic compounds that are similar to codeine and morphine which are equally effective (Table 3). There are also several synthetic narcotic analgesics that have a chemical structure different from opium derivatives. These include Demerol, Talwin, and

Table 3

Narcotic Analgesics

Generic	Brand Name	Method of Administration
Codeine*	Codeine	Tablets 30, 60 mg. Or by injection
Propoxyphene*	Darvon	Tablets 32, 65 mg
Meperidine	Demerol	Tablets 50, 100 mg. Or by injection
Morphine	Morphine	By injection
Hydromorphone	Dilaudid	Tablets 1, 2, 3, 4, 5, mg. Or by injection
Pentazocine*	Talwin	By injection
Methadone	Dolophine	Tablets 5, 10 mg. Or by injecction
Oxycodone	Oxycontin	Tables 10, 20, 40, 80 mg

* There are many combinations of codeine, synthetic drugs with similar effects, and Talwin with other medications. Examples include Percodan, Percocet, Vicodin, Damason-P, Darvon compund, Darvocet-N, and many others.

EFFECTS AND SIDE EFFECTS OF DRUGS

several other drugs. All these substances are called narcotics because they induce sleep and they also cause addiction.

Most of the narcotic agents have some uncomfortable side effects in some individuals. These include nausea, vomiting, drowsiness, and often itching, but they seldom produce serious side effects unless used in overdosage.

The danger of these agents is that of drug dependence. Drugs such as propoxyphene (Darvon) and codeine have a relatively low potential for producing addiction if they are not used over long periods of time. Some of the other drugs such as heroin, morphine, Dilaudid, and even Talwin can produce rapid onset of severe addiction. Addiction to these drugs is responsible for a major part of the crime in this country. Burglary, prostitution, and violent crimes occur because those who are addicted will do almost anything to obtain money to support their habit. These drugs are legally available by prescription only.

Antidepressants and tranquilizers.

Antidepressants are frequently used in treatment of either migraine or muscle-contraction headache. They can be quite effective for this purpose. Many people with chronic headache may become depressed because of the pain and also because of the serious adverse effect this symptom has on their lifestyle. In addition, many people who are depressed for some other reason experience a major problem with headache during their periods of depression. Antidepressants are also helpful in relieving headache in persons who are not depressed. For these reasons it can be expected that antidepressant medication will be beneficial in treatment of some persons with headache. These drugs probably produce their antiheadache effect by a drug action separate from their antidepressant effect in addition to relieving depression.

Tranquilizers that are often used for treatment of mental illness can also be helpful in treatment of headache in some cases. Drugs of this type include Thorazine, Stelazine, and Mellaril. It has been learned by clinical experience that a combination of an antidepressant medication and a tranquilizer is one of the best means of treating chronic pain syndromes regardless of what they are due to or what part of the body is affected. Chronic use may produce severe adverse reactions.

Depression does not appear to be a significant factor in the cause of either muscle-contraction headache or migraine in most people. Nevertheless, treatment with the above named drugs, of which there are many, often decreases headache even when no evidence of depression is present. Traditionally the most effective antidepressant drug for treatment of headache is amitriptyline (Elavil). This drug has a greater effect to prolong the action of serotonin in the brain than most of the other antidepressant medications. Since this effect on serotonin is different than that of many of the other anti-headache medications it is possible that it combats headache by another mechanism. Abnormalities of the effects of serotonin in the brain have long been considered a possible cause of headache.

The chief undesirable side effect of amitriptyline and similar drugs is sedation. When these agents are used at bedtime this is less of a problem and this effect can even be beneficial in inducing sleep. A major problem in use of these drugs may arise in some persons who have difficulty initiating urination. This is especially true of elderly men with enlargement of the prostate gland. Some of these persons have gone into acute urinary retention when these drugs were used. For this reason it is best to begin therapy with a small dose of medication to see if this or other side effects occur. Dry mouth occurs almost universally when these substances are used. Sometimes there is a tendency for persons who use these medications to gain weight. Some individuals who use these substances have a drop in blood pressure if they stand up quickly and this may even cause fainting. These drugs have to be used cautiously in persons with heart trouble because they increase the symptoms of some kinds of heart disease. They are available by prescription only.

There is another group of antidepressants that can be used to treat headache. The mechanism of action of these drugs is different from that of drugs like amitriptyline. These substances are called monoamine oxidase inhibitors. They have more side effects than drugs like amitriptyline. These medications have to be used very cautiously because of their toxic potential and their interactions with other substances. It is even dangerous to eat some kinds of cheese and some kinds of fish when these drugs are used because substances in these foods in the presence of monoamine oxidase inhibitors may cause severe elevation of blood pressure. The most commonly used monoamine oxidase inhibitors include phenelzine (Nardil) and tranylcypromine (Parnate). These drugs are used infrequently for treatment of headache. They are available by prescription only.

Sedatives and anti-anxiety drugs.

These drugs are not antiheadache medications in the

RELIEF FROM HEADACHE

Table 4

Antianxiety Drugs

Generic	Brand Name	Method of Administration
Diazepam	Valium	Tablets 2,5, 10 mg. Or by injection
Chlordiazepdoxide	Librium	Capsules 5, 10, 15 mg. Or by injection
Lorazepam	Ativan	Tablets 0.5, 1.0, 2.0 mg. Or by injection
Oxazepam	Serax	Tablets 10, 15, 30 mg
Alprazolam	Xanax	Tablets 0.25, 0.5, 1.0 mg
Clorazepate	Tranxene	Tablets 3.75, 7.5, 15 mg
Prazepam	Centrax	Tablets 5, 12, 20 mg
Phenobarbital	Phenobarbital	Tablets 15, 30, 60, 120. Or by injection
Meprobamate	Miltown, Equanil	Tablets 200, 400, 600 mg

usual sense but they are frequently given to persons with headache to decrease response to emotional pressure. This class of drugs includes Phenobarbital, Valium, Librium, Ativan, Meprobamate, Xanax, and similar medications (Table 4). Alcohol is also in this class. It has sometimes been said that the similarities between these drugs and alcohol are greater than their differences. All of these drugs, like alcohol, have a potential for causing dependency.

The benefit from these drugs probably depends chiefly on their ability to cause relaxation and decrease response to emotional stress. It is for this reason that they are called antianxiety drugs. Sedation to produce more restful sleep may also partially account for their effect. These drugs are not analgesics but they tend to increase the effect of narcotic analgesics such as demerol and codeine. Since there is a tendency to drug dependence they should not be used on a long

EFFECTS AND SIDE EFFECTS OF DRUGS

term basis.

The most common side effect of these drugs is drowsiness and if excessive medication is used nearly all the symptoms characteristic of intoxication by ethyl alcohol can occur. These include slurred speech, difficulty with vision, incoordination, unsteady gait, poor concentration, and in some cases inappropriate behavior. There is a tendency to have a need for increasing the dose to produce the same effect as tolerance develops. If large doses are used, sudden withdrawal occasionally causes seizures just as sudden withdrawal from alcohol produces this effect. These drugs are available by prescription only.

Beta blockers.

The best known drug in this group that is used for treatment of headache is propranolol (Inderal). Controlled studies have shown that Atenolol (Tenormin) and Nadolol (Corgard) are also effective. This group of drugs gets its name from the blocking effect they exert on the neurotransmitter norepinephrine at the site of certain nerve structures in blood vessels. These drugs find their greatest use in treatment of hypertension, but it was observed by some individuals who were treated with these drugs that headache decreased.[6] The beta blockers, chiefly Inderal, are recognized antiheadache medications. These drugs can also be used for treatment of tremor of the hands and head. They find an occasional use by persons who speak or perform on stage to counteract the effects of "stage fright." They do decrease anxiety and this may be the chief way in which they help headache rather than by their beta blocking effect on blood vessels. Table 5

RELIEF FROM HEADACHE

Table 5

Beta Blockers

Generic	Brand Name	Method of Administration
Propranolol*	Inderal	Tablets 10, 20, 40, 60, 80, 100 mg. Or by injection
Metoprolol	Lopressor	Tablets 50, 100 mg
Atenolol	Tenormin	Tablets 50, 100 mg
Nadolol	Corgard	Tablets 20, 40, 80, 120, 160 mg
Timolol	Blocadren	Tablets 5, 10 mg
Pindolol	Visken	Tablets 5, 10 mg

* Propranolol is the most commonly used beta blocker for headache. It is the only beta blocker that is FDA approved for this purpose.

lists several drugs in this group.

The chief side effects of these medications are a feeling of fatigue and in some individuals a feeling of depression. They should be used with caution in any person who is already depressed whether the depression is secondary to headaches or due to other factors. These drugs may have an adverse effect in persons with a history of lung disease, especially if they have had asthma attacks. These drugs may precipitate an attack of asthma in some of these people. Some kinds of heart disease can be made worse by these medications. These drugs are available by prescription only.

Calcium channel blockers.

This group of drugs is one of the newest that has been used for treatment of headache. Initially very optimistic

EFFECTS AND SIDE EFFECTS OF DRUGS

reports were given but as the effects of these drugs in management of headache have been observed over a longer period of time it appears that the number of people who are helped by them is very small. These drugs find their greatest usefulness in the treatment of some kinds of heart disease and in treatment of hypertension, but they have been used for a large number of other medical conditions. The mechanism of action in treatment of headache is not known but it has been suspected that this may be due to their effects on blood vessels caused by their release of serotonin. One of their effects is to block the action of serotonin. There are several drugs in this class but their contribution to management of headache is modest (Table 6).

Although these drugs cause many uncomfortable symptoms they are relatively safe because they don't cause very many serious side effects. They can, however, make some kinds of heart disease worse and they can produce an exces-

Table 6

Calcium Channel Blocking Drugs*

Generic	Brand Name	Method of adminisration
Verapamil	Calan	Tablets 80, 120 mg. Or by injection
Diltiazem	Cardizem	Tablets 30, 60 mg
Nifedipine	Procardia	Capsules 10, 20 mg
Nimodipine	Nimotop	Capsules 30 mg

* None are FDA approved for headache.

RELIEF FROM HEADACHE

sive drop in blood pressure, causing dizziness, lightheadedness, and even fainting. They are reported to cause headache in some people and in addition they produce weakness, nausea, vomiting, nervousness, shortness of breath, and several other uncomfortable symptoms. These drugs are available by prescription only.

Antihistamines and decongestants.

Antihistamines have found their greatest use in man-

Table 7

Antihistamines and Decongestants

Antihistamines

Generic	Brand Name	Method of administration
Diphenhydramine	Benadryl	Tablets 25, 50 mg. Or by injection
Promethazine*	Phenergan	Tablets 12.5, 25, 50 mg. Or by injection
Hydroxyzine*	Vistaril	Tablets 25, 50, 100 mg. or by injection
Chlorpheniramine	Chlor-Trimeton	Tablets 4 mg

Decongestants**

Phenylpropanolamine	Propagest	Tablets 25, 50 mg
Phenylephrine***	Neo-Synephrine	
Pseudoephedrine	Sudafed	Tablets 30, 60 mg

* These drugs are often injected along with Demerol and other narcotic analgesics to potentiate their analgesic effect.

** There are more than one hundred combinations of these decongestants mixed with other drugs including aspirin, Tylenol, and antihistamines that are used to treat colds and sinus headaches. These include such preparations as Sinu-Tab, Sine-Aids, Sine-Off, and Contac.

*** Marketed only in combination with other drugs.

agement of headache in individuals suspected of having sinusitis or allergy of the respiratory tract as a cause of this symptom. They counteract allergic responses. They are usually used along with a nasal decongestant which opens nasal pathways to make breathing easier. They also make sinus drainage more effective. Most of the antihistamines produce sedation so they may promote sleep and some of them are marketed as over-the-counter sleep medications. One of the antihistamines, cyproheptadine (Periactin), blocks the effect of serotonin. It also has some calcium channel blocking effect but unfortunately it isn't very effective for any kind of headache. On some occasions it has been beneficial for cluster headache — especially if used in combination with methysergide (Sansert). Adverse effects include sedation, dizziness, confusion, nervousness, hallucinations, and in a few persons convulsions — especially if the medication is taken in overdose. The same effects can occur from use of other antihistamines.

Decongestants are drugs that act to shrink mucous membranes and thus enhance sinus drainage. Most of these substances are also weak central nervous system stimulants and in this respect they are similar to amphetamine. They may cause wakefulness. Most over-the-counter cold medicines contain one of these drugs (Table 7) along with an antihistamine and an analgesic such as aspirin or acetaminophen.

Triptans.

This class of drugs is among the newest and most effective medications for treatment of migraine. The first one on the market was sumatriptan (Imitrex) which can be given by mouth, subcutaneously, or by nasal spray. Several other triptans are also available. These include rizatriptan (Maxalt), zolmitriptan (Zomig), and others. These drugs are given as acute treatment for migraine headaches. They are by prescription only because there is a potential for serious side effects. Occasional heart attacks and strokes have occurred after taking these medications but these complications are very uncommon when these medications are used according to directions. These drugs help around 60 to 75 percent of persons with migraine but their use is limited by side effects in some persons.

Antiepileptic drugs.

Divalproex (Depakote). This drug is a compound containing Valproic acid which is used chiefly in the treatment of epilepsy which is effective in some persons for prevention of headache. It is not used for treatment of an acute headache attack. It has caused occasional severe side effects including fatal liver failure, but this is very rare. More common and less severe side effects include nausea and vomiting, drowsiness, tremor, dizziness, itching, and transient hair loss. Several other anti-epileptic drugs are also being used for treatment of headache.

Botulinum toxin (Botox).

This drug is given by injection only and is used primarily to treat some neurological conditions which cause abnormal muscle spasm and it is also used cosmetically for injection into the facial muscles to counteract wrinkles. Some persons report that it decreases or eliminates their headache for a period of a few weeks to a few months. This substance is very expensive, but a few people say that it is more effective for treatment of headache than any other treatment they have used.

Miscellaneous drugs used for treatment of headache.

The fact that so many drugs are used for treatment of headache suggests that no one drug or group of drugs provides the answer to this problem. The number of drugs that have been used for this purpose is too large to list but there are some other medications that are used in specific instances that will be briefly mentioned here.

1. Lithium. Lithium is an element but it had not been used medicinally until the 1950s when it was found to be effective against some kinds of mental disease. It is used for bipolar psychosis (manic depressive psychosis) which is characterized by fluctuations of mood from profound depression to manic states in which the person is very active and oftentimes manifests unreasonable and very hyperactive behavior. It was found serendipitously that Lithium can be of benefit in some cases to prevent attacks of cluster headaches and this is its main use in the headache arena (see chapter 11).

2. Prednisone. This is a synthetic drug that acts like cortisone which is effective in some cases to prevent cluster headache. Prednisone has a large number of undesirable side effects so it is usually not used for a long period of time for treatment of any kind of headache. It may be used initially to help get cluster headache under control, after which other drugs can be used.

RELIEF FROM HEADACHE

3. Papaverine. This drug comes from the opium poppy which is the same source that morphine and heroine come from. It is reported to be effective in some patients with migraine.

4. Oxygen inhalation. Breathing of 100 percent oxygen at a rate of 8 liters per minute for 5 to 10 minutes may abort headaches in some individuals. Persons who get best results are those who have cluster headache, classic migraine, or headache due to impaired respiratory function in which insufficient oxygen is delivered to the brain.

Many medications can give symptomatic relief from headache at least temporarily but best management consists of removal of the cause of this symptom so ongoing treatment with medication is not necessary. This is not always possible but up to ninety percent of persons with chronic headache who do not have serious disease can be helped by the measures described in chapter 2 if they follow the instructions correctly.

Index

RELIEF FROM HEADACHE

Acupuncture, 21, 74, 76, 142
Addiction, 46, 198, 199, 213
Aneurysm, 103, 105, 106
Anger, 11, 53, 63, 121, 161
Angiography, 92, 107
Arthritis, 12, 28, 57, 136
Biofeedback, 21, 74, 142
Blood vessels, 7, 9, 11, 29, 35, 58, 99, 103, 131, 168, 187, 203
Botox, 222
Brain tumors, 5, 29, 56, 87
Brain abscess, 5, 111, 114
Cerebrospinal fluid, 88, 94, 98, 100, 109
Chemicals, 9, 11, 124, 126
Chiropractic, 21, 45, 48, 74, 76, 141
Classification of headache, (*See Headache*)
Computed tomography (CT or CAT scanning), 22, 92, 93, 106, 132
Cranial nerves, 7, 178, 181
Depression, 50, 61, 90, 161, 214
Disability, 83, 165
Diseases, 166-174
Drugs, 19, 25, 74, 153
    antidepressants, 51, 73, 138, 213
    antihistamines, 202, 220
    aspirin, 4, 51, 84, 202, 207
    beta blockers, 217
    Cafergot, 20, 135
    caffeine, 137, 202
    codeine, 73, 211
    decongestants, 220

Demerol, 212, 216
Depakote, 138, 222
Dilaudid, 212
Elavil, 73, 76, 84, 126, 138
ergot, 19, 76, 134, 203
ibuprofen, 208, 210
Imitrex, 51, 132, 148, 221
lithium, 223
Maxalt, 51, 132, 148, 221
Midrin, 136
morphine, 212
Neurontin, 138
opium, 211
oral contraceptives, 130
Prednisone, 152, 171, 223
sedatives, 215
Thorazine, 214
tranquilizers, 51, 76, 213
triptans, 51, 221
Tylenol, 4, 84, 126, 211
Valium, 35, 51, 73, 215, 216
vasoconstrictors, 205, 220
Zomig, 51, 132, 148, 221
Drug dependence, 19, 26, 50, 73, 76, 136, 148, 202
Emotions, 13, 15, 21, 26, 50, 59, 64, 129, 160
Encephalitis, 112
Epileptic seizures, 181, 199
Essentials, 40
Evil spirits, 16
Exercise, 54, 75
Fascia, 9, 69
Fibrous tissue, 8, 27, 30, 33, 37, 64
Food allergy, 41, 128, 194
Glaucoma, 90, 175
Headache, Classification of,

INDEX

10, 63
  chronic daily, 148
  cluster, 5, 90, 148, 150
  migraine, 1, 6, 11, 63,115-149, 154
  muscle-contraction, 5, 11, 15, 33, 72, 90
  myofascial, 5, 11, 69, 71
  psychogenic, 11, 61, 70, 72, 74, 157, 161
  tension, 11, 14, 26, 62, 70
Head injury, 28, 79, 96
Hemorrhage, 5, 8, 29, 56, 95
  epidural, 96
  subarachnoid, 98
  subdural, 97
Herniated discs, 12, 64, 170
High blood pressure, 101, 167
Hyperextension, 83
Hypertension, 101, 168
Hypochondriasis, 162
Infections, 108
Insurance, 83, 164
Laugh therapy, 55
Lifestyle, change in, 55, 140, 164
Ligaments, 27
Litigation, 26, 47, 50, 165
Lumbar puncture, 195, 197
Magnetic resonance imaging (MRI), 22, 92, 93, 106
Maneuver, 40, 42, 56
Medication, 35, 133, 134
Meningitis, 5, 7, 9, 18, 29, 56, 109, 110
Migraine, 1, 6, 11, 63
Mobility, 27, 29, 34, 39
Monosodium glutamate, 128, 141
Murphy's Law, 44
Muscle spasm, 28, 54, 65
Neck, 27, 29, 33, 39, 41, 49, 56, 65, 67
Neck collar, 53, 84
Neuralgia, 181, 182, 183
Nitrates, 128
Non-compliance, 42, 45
Over-the-counter, 19, 73, 76
Oxygen, 9, 139, 153, 167, 187, 223
Pain, 1, 8, 90, 159, 164, 165, 175, 181,
Pain-sensitive, 6, 7, 8, 88, 90, 95, 197
Pharmacotherapy, 74
Physical therapy, 50, 75, 85
Placebo, 16, 19
Postconcussion, 81
Psychiatric treatment, 21, 47, 85
Range of motion, 28, 29, 43, 84
Relaxation, 51, 53, 74
Secondary gain, 71, 164
Serotonin, 125, 126, 206, 214, 216
Sinusitis, 178
Skull, 6, 8, 82, 169
Stretching, 39, 40, 43, 46
Stroke, 160, 171, 172
Temporomandibular joint (TMJ) 38, 180
Trephination, 17
Vertebrae, 27, 28, 169, 184

About the Author

Donald I. Peterson, M.D., FACP, FAAN, is a neurologist who recently retired as Professor of Neurology and Associate Professor of Pharmacology at Loma Linda University School of Medicine, Loma Linda, California. Dr. Peterson is a clinician and medical research investigator who is the author of nearly 70 scientific papers.

Over the last thirty years he has successfully treated many persons with chronic headache including many who were diagnosed with migrane but who failed to get relief from traditional medical management. Many persons, even those with daily headache, became headache free if they followed the instructions in this book correctly and consistantly.

Dr. and Mrs. Peterson have three children, one of whom is also a neurologist.